Family Ghosts

The Jackson Family Haunting

By Rick and William Jackson

ISBN: 978-1-7366130-0-9

This book is dedicated to the Jackson Family. For those that are gone and those that remain.

Introduction

The house is unimpressive, a modest two-story farmhouse that most people would drive by without even a second look. It is a small house. Although two stories, the house is under one thousand square feet, including the bathroom and back hallway added to the house during the renovation of the 1980s. For many years, the house did not have running water. Financial trouble and a dried-up well forced the family to carry water in jugs up the hill from the cabin they once lived in for cooking, washing, and cleaning. Everything depended on the stream of water from the bottom of the hill to the top carried in old washed-out milk jugs. Poverty rested upon the family for many years. Mama and Daddy sat, watching others go out to lunch at restaurants while they ate what they could scrape together from a brown paper bag. The kids at times wore shoes made up more of cardboard and duct tape than rubber and canvas. For most people, living in the house would have seemed like a really difficult experience. Still, for the Jackson family, it was just home.

Robert and Kathy raised their three kids there - Bud, Tracy, and Ricky. The little white farmhouse was a vibrant place with laughter and happiness for the most part. Like all families, sadness crept in as often as it could, but they held together. Growing up in the old house allowed the kids to discover things about themselves that most of their friends would not know until they were older. Hard work and perseverance were mandatory for the kids. Everyone had to be involved with making it work. To see the family interact, you would see a normal family. They fought and laughed and loved together in that house. They appreciated the good times they shared. When they all grew up and became adults, they could handle adversity when others around them floundered because they had seen worse times.

The house to them seemed normal, but there was something else there. There was something under the surface of the house that few experienced, but that brought the family closer together as shared experiences do. The house was most definitely haunted. With each member of the family having experienced something, it helped to bind them. Reading the following stories, it would be easy to think of the house as a terrifying place. If all of these things had happened in a short period of time, that would be the case. It should be stressed, though, at the very beginning that these experiences happened over the course of many years. The house was bought in 1986 and is still lived in by family members to this very day. So, all of these stories took place over the course of several decades. Something might happen today in the house. Then, there may be several years in between that experience and the next experience.

The house was the anchor, but not only did the family experience hauntings there, but they also experienced paranormal activity seemingly wherever they went. Did the house flip some kind of switch in them? This normal, all-American family suddenly found themselves as conduits to the other side, where they found themselves becoming sensitive to spirits and other phenomena. It was not a new phenomenon that the family had been in contact with the paranormal; there had been many stories passed down through the family's history. There seemed to be something about the family; some open window that they could see through when others could not.

Chapter 1

"Everything is connected and touches everything else. Like a stone tossed into a pond, the ripples expand far beyond what the eyes can perceive."

Gravier's Bookshop by Evelyn Klebert

The pine logs popped and crackled in the fire pit, creating a mushroom of warmth in the crisp October air. Gathered around the fire were friends and family that had come together to celebrate Halloween in what had been a challenging year for everyone. Kids sat on parents' laps and snuggled in tightly, and men put their arms around their wives as they watched the flames leap over the charred logs in red and orange flames. The light gently illuminated the white siding of the little farmhouse that connected them all in some way. Woods surrounded them on all other sides, and a full moon showed through the trees behind them. Lights appeared through the trees, and the sound of the diesel tractor that Bud was driving began to rumble towards the group, drowning out their conversations.

They watched as it came near, carrying the last group of the night on the "haunted woods tour" that Bud had put together. He had wanted to make it as special as possible for the kids since so much had been taken from them due to the ongoing COVID-19 pandemic. He had spent days buying Halloween decorations and hanging them strategically in the trees. A graveyard of Styrofoam headstones and skeletons had been constructed, and spotlights were placed around the woods to illuminate hanging scarecrows and werewolves. One group at a time had loaded into the trailer behind the tractor, and he drove them through dark roads and woods where noise-activated ghosts and ghouls would chatter and boo them. As the last group appeared, the sound of laughter overtook the sound of the tractor, and Ricky appeared out of the darkness, shirtless and brushing dirt from his knees. In the spirit of the grand finale, he had taken off his shirt, exposing his ample gut and hairy chest and back. Then, he ran through the dark woods ahead of the tractor, activating the hanging ghosts. He had stumbled and fell as they went past him but rolled over and continued his mission until they had gotten the best show of all. It had been hilarious.

Bud pulled the tractor to a stop and wiped tears from his eyes.

"I could hardly see straight," he said through chuckles. "I was laughing so hard!"

"What are you doing with your shirt off?" was the main question from the fire crowd.

"He had his shirt off running through the woods," Lauren, Bud's daughter, said, barely able to speak.

"He fell and rolled over so many times! He was so white he looked like a ghost!" they howled with laughter.

Ricky put on his shirt as the riders of the last tour related the events of the last ride. Bud walked by him on the way to the food table, where he got a cup of hot apple cider. Ricky followed him, and they stood off to the side together for a moment and looked at their family, laughing and having a great time. It needed not be said that they were happy to be there all together. Family was so important to them both, and roots meant the world to them. The trees, the rocks, and the dirt surrounding them were just as much a part of them as their right hand. Their lives were woven into the land, and it spoke to them.

"It is getting late," Ricky said. "I think the kids have about had it."

"Yeah," Bud said. "They look worn out."

"I am going to tell a ghost story, and then we will go."

Bud nodded in agreement.

Ricky stepped into the firelight. "Can I have everyone's attention, please?" He waited a moment until the talking died down and all eyes were on him.

"Since it is Halloween and it is getting late, I figured that I would send you all home with a ghost story."

He took a sip of his warm apple cider and put it down on the arm of the Adirondack chair where he was sitting earlier. To build suspense, he took a moment to look around the fire as each person was staring at him in anticipation.

"This happened to me a long time ago now. It was soon after Meghan and I got married. Probably about sixteen to seventeen years ago. I was an Assistant Manager at the grocery store at the time, and I had just gotten transferred to the small, old store that is near the mall in Raleigh." He watched as everyone nodded, indicating that they knew exactly the location he was talking about.

"I had been transferred there because the store was really in bad shape. It wasn't so much the guy I was replacing that had the store in a mess. The Store Manager was not a great leader, and the department managers that she had were very poor. The weakest link was a guy named Roger, who was the grocery department manager. He was a really big guy, and I mean a REALLY BIG guy." Ricky held his hands out to his side, demonstrating the size of Roger. "He had to weigh about four hundred pounds at least, so already he was going to have trouble navigating such a physical job, but to make matters worse, he worked overnight by himself.

Before I transferred there, the store had been a twenty-four-hour store, which meant that they were always open. Roger had worked the overnight shift of 11pm to 7am the next morning. When the company changed the store's hours to being only opened from 7am to 11pm, the store manager had let him continue to work overnight by himself because of childcare issues with his wife's schedule. That wasn't even the big problem. The big problem was that he would not do anything!

I would leave him lists or leave things loaded up on carts with signs on them directing him what to do, but I would find everything as I had left it when I came in the next day. The only evidence that I ever had that he was there was the empty Mountain Dew bottles and bags of chips in the trashcan in the store's office. Magazines were always easily found stuffed behind the computer in there where he would obviously camp out overnight and watch the clock tick by. To say it was frustrating was an understatement. I would complain to the Store Manager and try to write him up, but she liked him and always protected him. Finally, I decided that if I could not fire him, I would just make his life miserable.

So, one night when he came in to work at 11pm, I was ready to give him some great news. I had worked since 1pm that afternoon, but I informed him that I was going to run home and change clothes, then I was going to come back and work overnight with him. It was not really a big deal to me. I was young and had no kids. I was off the next day, and Meghan had to work, so I was just going to be hanging around anyway. No big deal!

I could see the disappointment on his face as I am sure he had plans to read swimsuit magazines and to eat Cheetos all night in the office. True to my word, I went home and grabbed a bite to eat and changed clothes. When I got back to the store an hour or so later, the parking lot was deserted, and just Roger's car remained. I had to let myself into the store because the doors were locked, and sure enough, I found him on his stool in the office looking at the computer. It was clear that he was not excited about the situation, but he and I went to work.

For the next few hours, we toiled all around the store. By the early morning hours, maybe three or four in the morning, we were on the back-loading dock stacking boxes and cleaning. The loading dock was a large room with two roll-up doors on one side and shelves, or "bunkers" as we called them, filled with product against the walls. There was a large opening into an even bigger backroom where the breakroom was and more bunkers. I could see partially into the bigger back room from where I was standing, and I could see the mop closet and the meat department doors, which were stainless steel swinging doors, to my left. Roger was across from me behind where I was standing to my left when suddenly I noticed movement from the corner of my eye. I looked up in enough time to see a man walk from the back room into the meat department. I watched as he disappeared through the doors, and they swung on their hinges.

'Sir,' I called after him and followed him into the meat department. When I entered the room, I could see that it was empty. 'What was this guy doing in here?' I thought. Many scenarios ran through my mind. Was it some contractor that was here to work on something that I didn't know about? Was it a customer that had wandered into the store? Had I left the door unlocked?

I knew that unless I had left the door unlocked, anyone else would have had to contact me to get into the store. When I emerged from the dark meat department, I looked up and down the back aisle, but the store was empty. I walked on to the produce department and then checked the sales floor. The front doors were locked, I discovered as I came around the front end, and while I was there, I looked under the cash registers. Nothing! I checked the office and came down the dairy aisle heading back towards the back room. As I got to the lady's room, it suddenly hit me.

'Where the Hell is Roger?!' I thought.

I began to get angry as I searched in the bathroom stalls and then in the men's room. As I came through the doors of the back room, I was seething with anger. Was he so damn lazy that he wouldn't even back me up when there was someone in the store in the middle of the night? I checked the breakroom, and I came back around to where I had started. Sure enough, there was Roger. He had not moved an inch the entire time. I laid into him something fierce.

'Hey man, what the Hell are you doing? I could be getting murdered right now on the cereal aisle,' I said, staring a hole through him as he paid me little attention and continued to stack the boxes I had told him to earlier. It just made me angrier as I watched him for a moment. 'Now he wants to work,' I thought.

'Roger, are you listening to me?' I yelled, 'Didn't you see the man in the store?' I asked.

'I see him all the time,' he replied, not straying from his task or looking up at me at all.

I stood dumbfounded at what he had just said to me. As his words washed over me, I began to realize truly what he was saying.

'He sees him all of the time,' I thought. What had just happened settled into my brain as things seemed to go into slow motion, and my mind went into hyperdrive. I thought about what he said and could see that he had not necessarily been sitting in the office because he was lazy; he was hiding out. He was scared. It dawned on me that I was scared too. I had been perfectly willing to face a flesh and blood man that was in the store, but what the Hell did he mean he sees him all of the time?

"Roger," I said again, this time in a calm and lower voice. He stopped his stacking and looked at me in the eyes.

"I will see you tomorrow," I said, and I turned around and left him standing there."

Everyone around the fire giggled at the punch line as Ricky picked up his cider and took another sip.

"I let myself out of the store, locking the door behind me, went home, and got into bed. I never told Meghan what happened because I thought maybe I was crazy or she would think I was. I was a little easier on him after that but never became a huge Roger fan. When he asked for a transfer a few months later, I gladly endorsed the move and brought in my own guy. The overnight visitor that I had seen was never mentioned between us again. A few years later, my mother-in-law was transferred to the store where I had seen the man, and I was working at the bank. One day she was at my house, and we were talking.

She said, 'You like ghost stories, right?'

'I do,' I told her.

'Well, you should talk with this lady I work with. She is the Grocery Manager and closes the store five nights a week. She told me sometimes she sees a man in the store, but then he will just be gone.' It wasn't till I heard this that I ever told anyone what had happened to me."

When Ricky finished, everyone looked at each other with a smile. "What a great ending to a Halloween party," they were thinking. The older kids ran up to him with a million questions.

"What happened to Roger? What if the guy just lived in the store and never told anyone?" they asked.

From over their voices, Ricky heard his oldest Niece's husband say, "Man, y'all are some ghost seeing people. I have never been around people that had seen as many ghosts and have so many ghost stories."

Bud had heard it too, and he and Ricky knowingly looked at each other. Ricky looked back over his shoulder at the old white farmhouse that looked back at him as if it knew the answer. They did have a lot of ghost stories. He knew from personal experience that they had, but why? He had once heard someone say that there was no haunted house, just haunted people. Maybe he was right.

Chapter 2

The Jackson family came to the Piedmont of North Carolina through the same route that many other Scots-Irish families did. Seemingly always restless, their ancestors left Southern Scotland and Northern England for the Ulster Plantation of Ireland. They brought hopes of a new beginning but also brought their restlessness and soon found themselves on ships embarking on a grand adventure to the new world of America. The port of Philadelphia welcomed them, but soon they headed south to the fertile fields of Orange County, North Carolina, where they stayed until the late 1890s. Reconstruction had been hard on the farmers of the south. The uncertainty of growing crops in an ever-changing political climate drove them into the city where textile mills offered steady work and steady pay.

The first indication of a "sixth sense" that has been told throughout the years was of a distant uncle born with a veil, or caul, over his face. This is a thin layer of skin that wraps around a baby. It is easily removed by the doctor and causes no physical damage to the child. Still, for the old wives, it is a sign of a spiritual difference. It is said that children born in this manner have a deeper connection to the other side and can see things that others cannot see. They know things that have not happened yet, and it is said that they cannot drown. It is said that throughout his life, he would seem intuitive to things about to take place, and he would see things. Strange things.

He often told the story that in the early 1930s, he would ride a bus into town to work, and he would work late into the night often. The bus would take him to the end of the line on the very outskirts of the city, but then he would have to walk through the night for quite a distance to get home. One night the bus stopped, and he walked to the open doors where the city street turned into a dirt road heading back into the countryside. One lonely street light illuminated the bus stop, and as he stood on the steps of the bus, he saw a woman in a fine dress sitting on a bull under the light. He stopped and looked slowly over his shoulder at the driver who was holding the door handle, waiting for him to get off.

"Surely he can see her," he thought, but the driver just looked at him.

"You alright, buddy?" the driver asked.

He looked back to the woman who stared at him with an expressionless face, and the restless bull shifted under her as if wanting to charge off into the night but restrained.

"Yeah," he said as he took a step off onto the road.

As he stood there, he heard the air brakes squeal behind him, and the engine of the bus roared and pulled away. The sound of the motor faded as he stood staring at the woman who stared back at him. When silence descended upon him, he could hear only the breathing of the bull.

"She is not real," he told himself as he began to walk towards her down the street. He never took his eyes off of her, nor did she him as he came closer to her. When he came abreast to her, he stopped and looked up at her.

"Ma'am, it is not safe for a lady to be out here at this time of night." She just looked down at him with no expression. "I would get down off of that bull if I was you," he said. "Bulls are ornery animals, and he might throw you." Again, she just looked at him. Finally, he broke her gaze and turned to begin his walk home. He could feel her watching him as he walked into the darkness. He knew she was a spirit, and speaking to her helped to ease his fear, but he still felt a slow-moving terror that seemed to rise up from his feet as he walked, compelling him to run. As he was about to run for home, he looked once more over his shoulder to find that she was gone. He breathed a sigh of relief but would find that many nights he would get off the bus to the same woman who would watch him walk past. Every night he would speak to her to try to ease his fear, and every night he would find that she was gone when he looked back over his shoulder for her.

Clifton Jackson was the first to move his family to town. He settled his family in a mill house near the Erwin Cotton Mill in West Durham, where they would spend the next few generations. Births, deaths, wars, and economic depression would come and go in the world. Family would be scattered at times but seemed to always come back to the cotton mill and to the familiar streets of West Durham. Clifton's son, Willie, and his wife, Lee, settled there too, and he worked as an electrician in the mill alongside many of his relatives. It was a hard life, but it was better than life on the farm had been. Willie and Lee had a son named Robert, and when Robert was two years old, Lee became pregnant again. She and Willie welcomed a baby girl named Elizabeth, and life was good in the little mill house. She would watch her husband leave for work every day, walk to the mill, and then begin her work as a homemaker and mother, cooking, cleaning, and taking care of the kids. One day, the baby got sick, but the doctor told her it was nothing to be concerned about. It was just a normal childhood sickness that she would work through.

One night as everyone in the house slept, she retreated to bed after a long day of work. The dishes were washed, and the house was clean and ready for another day as she lay beside her husband, looking up at the ceiling in the darkness. Soon she had fallen into a deep sleep. She was brought out of sleep by the sound of music. Thinking she was dreaming at first, she lay in the bed listening. She closed her eyes to try to locate the source of the music. It was the most beautiful music she had ever heard in her life - a symphony of string instruments playing an angelic tune. She got out of bed and began to walk around the house but could not find where the music was coming from. She opened the front door and stepped out on the porch. The night was silent and still, but behind her, from the house, she could hear the music continue to play.

Lee decided to check on the baby since she was up and headed to her room. As she entered the room, the music abruptly stopped. She stopped, and even though the music had been such a mystery just a moment before, the silence now unnerved her. She made her way over to the crib and bent over to check on the baby. She laid her hand across the baby's small body and immediately knew that she was gone. She picked up her lifeless daughter and held her close to her as she began to cry. Her precious daughter was dead. Until her death, over sixty years later, she swore that the music she heard was the music of the angels coming to take her baby girl home.

Some years later, on a hot July day years later, most of the family was working first-shift at the mill. After supper, they sought the relief of the shade as a reprieve from the heat on their front porch. As they sat on the porch, they would look up and down the street and see who was coming and going from the mill and from town. On that July evening, they all saw Rosa Jackson coming down the street towards them from the mill. Clifton, her dad, announced to everyone that she must be on break and coming home to grab a bite to eat as he rocked back and forth in his chair. They all nodded in agreement at the statement. Second-shift was tough, and they had all worked it before. It would not be out of place for her to come home and eat just to get out of the loud and dusty weave room where she worked.

As she drew closer, they could see that she had a strange look on her face. She was just walking, looking straight ahead as if in a daze. They watched her come closer to the house, then get to the house, and then continue walking right past them. She never even looked over at them.

"Rosa," her dad called to her. "Rosa," but she kept on walking past them. Clifton went after her knowing that something must be wrong with her. He ran down the steps and out into the street where he saw that she was gone. Although she had just been there, and they had all seen her, now he looked down an empty street at nothing. He took off his hat and looked back at the other family members who were sitting on the porch, wondering what had just happened. He scratched his head and walked back to his seat on the porch, where he sat for the rest of the night. As the evening went on, they talked about what had happened, and as time passed, people left and went home or went to bed, but Clifton stayed there in his chair.

He was unnerved by what had happened, and his anxiety was at a fevered pitch when just in time, he saw the outline in the darkness of Rosa coming down the street when her shift was over. She saw him sitting there and ran to him like she always did. He was so happy to see her, and he told her what happened. She hadn't left the mill all day, she told him, and laughed.

"You must be going crazy," she said. He was not laughing and insisted she had walked by and that everyone had seen her. They went back and forth for a time, but finally, she convinced him that she had not left the mill her entire shift.

"Ok," he finally relented, but something was not right; he knew.

Less than a week later, the family stood in the pouring rain around a hole in the ground and a coffin at a small country church. They watched as gravediggers tried desperately to keep the water from filling the hole with buckets and then lowered the coffin into the muddy orange water that they had failed to drain. Clifton put his hand on the shoulder of his small red-haired grandson, who looked up at him. The pouring rain could not hide his tears, and Clifton pulled him closer to him. He couldn't help but wonder as they laid his daughter to rest if somehow her spirit had begun to wander even before she was dead.

For four generations, the Jacksons would stalk the halls of the cotton mill - Clifton, Willie, Robert, and then his son Robert Junior. It was rare occasions when there was a break in continuity. Willie found himself in his late thirties serving in the United States Navy after the Japanese attacked Pearl Harbor. An older man, and skilled electrician, he was one of the very first Sea Bees, who were combat engineers that the Navy used to secure islands and build airstrips and facilities in the Pacific theater. His son Robert also served in the Navy as a Gunner's Mate on destroyers in Europe and the Mediterranean. By the late 1940s, though, they found themselves back in the familiar halls of the mill.

For Robert, it was a fortunate move. It was not long until he spotted Mildred Carden working the looms. She was at first uninterested in the obviously smitten young man. He came by as often as he could find an excuse and would bring her a drink or a snack that he bought her from the cafeteria. Their relationship escalated to him giving her rides home after work, and pretty soon, they were in love. They settled into the same routine that had been traditional for the family; work at the mill, live in a mill house and start a family.

They had three children, two girls and a boy. The boy was Robert Junior. He was a typical boy of the early 1960s, and West Durham was his playground. He rode his bike, played baseball, and knew everyone everywhere in the world of west Durham. Life on "Mill Hill" was spartan, but the people were happy. His childhood was rarely penetrated by sadness, but one day when he was little, heartache shattered his little world. A man came to their door and asked to speak to his dad outside. Robert Junior sat on a chair in the kitchen as his mom washed dishes. She pretended not to be worried about the muffled conversation her husband was having outside of the window, but he could tell she was worried. When his dad came back into the house, she stopped washing and looked at her husband.

"Well, I think my daddy has gotten himself into something that he can't get out of this time," he said.

He was right. Willie Jackson had survived the great depression, fighting in the war, and a life of hard living. He had gone on a hunting trip in eastern North Carolina with a friend, and the last person to see them saw the boat they were in turn over. It took several days of dragging the water for their bodies to be found. Robert Junior was devastated and never would forget his grandpa and the short time they had together. Lee was heartbroken and found solace in her little grandson. Robert Junior would be a grandma's boy for the rest of her life, always feeling like he had to watch out for her as if his grandpa had left him this task.

Chapter 3

The summer of 1969 was a hot one in Durham. The Vietnam war was raging, man was moving closer to walking on the moon, and racial tensions in the south were reaching an all-time high. Robert Junior had been playing baseball with his friends and was dying of thirst. He was walking back home and could see his front porch. In his mind, he was crawling through the desert parched and had just seen an oasis. He picked up speed at the thought of a cool glass of water and began to run the last couple of blocks. He busted through the front door and made his way through the house to the kitchen. His dad was working second-shift at the mill. His mom was at Watt's Hospital recovering from gall bladder surgery, so he and his two sisters had their run of the house until later in the evening when their grandparents would come and stay with them until their dad got home from work late in the night.

The plan had been for them to stay there by themselves, but the first night they were home alone, they had a scare. Their dad had left and made sure that Mildred Lee, the oldest, knew that she was to have everyone home before dark and that she was not to open the door for anyone under any circumstances. She was a responsible girl, and he knew that he could count on her. After school, she laid down the law to her brother and sister and made sure everyone was on the same page. They knew better than to try her. If they survived her wrath, they knew that she would escalate the situation to the big boss, dad, and he would apply some leather belt therapy to get them on track. Even at their ages, their dad would still not spare the rod and spoil the child. Night fell, and the three kids watched television together and then went to bed as they had been told. Shortly after all of the lights were out, they began to hear knocking on the front door. They met in the hall where they could see the front door and the silhouette of a man on the other side of the door through the glass. They stood back from the door watching from the hall, not knowing who it could be or what he could want so late. The knocking became a beating on the door, and they wondered if the man would break the door down.

Just as soon as he appeared at the door, he disappeared. They waited in the silence of the house for a few moments, and then Robert Junior crept to the window and peered out to the empty porch. When Robert got home, he was mad to find them all awake and in the living room with the lights on. As he opened his mouth to yell at them, though, they ran across the room and embraced him. When they told him what happened, he knew he had to make sure they were not left alone again. He arranged for his in-laws, Buck and Ruby, to come over as soon as they could the next night, which was just before dark, and they would wait until he got home to leave.

Robert Junior didn't mind them coming by. He enjoyed the little bit of freedom that he had after school every day. He took a quick turn down the hall to his room and threw his glove on his bed. As he turned back to the hall, he stopped and looked back into his room. Standing in the corner was an old man, bent over at the waist as if he had a bad back. He had a full white beard. Robert Junior locked eyes with him for just a moment and then blinked. The old man was suddenly gone. He rubbed his eyes.

"I must be seeing things," he thought. He went into the kitchen and drank two glasses of water in front of the kitchen sink. He looked around the room as if he was waiting for someone to jump out at him at any moment. He decided that he should go outside and see who he could find to hang out with in the neighborhood until his sisters got home.

Later, when his grandparents arrived, he waited until his sisters were not in the room and told his grandparents what he had seen.

Grandma Ruby told him that his mind was just playing tricks on him because he had such a scare when they were home alone. "There couldn't have been a man in your room, Robert Junior," she said.

"I guess you are right," he said.

"No," Grandpa Buck broke in, "I saw him too." Both Robert Junior and his grandma looked at his grandpa with surprise.

"A few nights ago, when I was visiting," he began, "I was sitting in that chair," he pointed to Robert's chair at the head of the living room. From the chair, you could see the television and down the hall to the bedrooms.

"Something caught my eye down the hall after you kids went to bed, and we were waiting for your daddy. I thought one of you kids was up, but when I looked down the hall, I saw a man walk out of your room. He was a bent old man, just like you described, and had a beard. He stopped in the middle of the hall and turned and looked at me. We looked at each other for a few seconds, and then he disappeared. I didn't say anything to anyone because I knew that what I saw was not flesh and blood."

They couldn't believe it, but Grandpa Buck was an honest man. They agreed that there was no need to tell anyone else what they had seen because it would just scare the other kids or make Robert worry while he was at work. In a few days, their mom came home from the hospital, and the man was never seen again. He only appeared in the few days that their mom was gone.

When Robert Junior finally told his mom and dad about what happened, it was many years later after they had moved. Nothing odd had ever gone on in the house, and they were skeptical. They confirmed the story with Grandma Ruby since Grandpa Buck had already passed away. They knew Robert Junior would not lie, but they still felt that he was just seeing things. They remained skeptics for the rest of their lives, but Mildred did have an experience years later that she could not explain.

In 1977, they moved onto the land where Robert's mother, Lee, lived in Eastern Durham County. She had bought the land after Willie died and would live there until her death in 1989. The years had passed, and Mildred and Robert had become Granny and Pop. Pop was still working at the cotton mill and had a long drive to get downtown from the country. He had to be there at 6:30am, so he had to be up by 5am to get ready and get there. Because of this, he went to bed pretty early. Most nights, he left Granny up watching television by herself until she finished the 11 o'clock news, and then she would go to bed.

One night after Pop had gone to bed, she was at the kitchen sink finishing the dishes from supper. Standing at the sink, she was staring straight down the hallway to her bedroom door. She heard the door open and looked down the hall to see Pop come out of the door and go into the hallway bathroom. She had a question that she had forgotten to ask him and figured that she would ask him when he came out of the bathroom since he was up. She waited and waited and waited for him to come out, but he never did. She realized that he had been in there for quite a while, and as she put the last dish in the drying rack, she got concerned about him.

She wiped her hands on her apron and walked across the living room and down the back hall.

"Robert!" she called. There was no answer. She opened the bathroom door and found the room empty. She stood for a second running through her mind the sequence of events. "He should be here," she thought. She continued down the hall and opened the bedroom door. "Robert," she called out again as she opened the door. As the light of the hallway lit up the room where she could see her bed and the distinct lump under the covers that was her husband, she asked, "Did you get up and go to the bathroom?" Pop's face appeared, one eye squinted at the light and a cowlick forming on the side of his head. Obviously, being awakened from a deep sleep, he hoarsely and annoyedly replied, "No, no, I haven't been up."

"Ok, sorry," she said as she backed out of the room. She went back into the living room and sat in her chair, pondering what she had seen. Nothing like that had ever happened in her whole life. She was sure that she had seen and heard Pop, no question about that. But he had obviously not been out of bed either. She sat in her chair, wringing her hands long after the news went off that night, and the television turned into a test pattern. No matter how she looked at what happened, she could not figure any good explanation. Had she been in her chair watching television, she could have blamed it on dozing off and dreaming, but she was washing dishes at the sink when it happened. There was no way she lost track of time. It was just the two of them, so they had just a few dishes to wash. Finally, she cut the lights off and went to bed. She never figured out a good explanation and never said she had seen a ghost, but she told the story for the rest of her life. It was always with a curiosity about what it could have been that had come out of the room and went into the bathroom that night.

Chapter 4

"Way back in my memory, there's a scene that I recall of a little run-down cabin in the woods. Where my daddy never promised that our blue moon would turn gold, but he lay awake nights wishing that it would."

"A Sharecroppers Dream"
By The Nitty Gritty Dirt Band

It was at E.K. Powe Elementary School where he first saw her - a little brown-haired girl with blue eyes named Kathy Tripp. Robert Junior, just plain old Robert to Kathy, had been held back a year, and he would always say it was the best thing that ever happened to him. He was smitten from the very start. Kathy was born in Havelock, North Carolina and was the baby of a family of five kids. Much like the Jacksons had been several generations before, the Tripp family was transient. Living in Havelock, Carrboro, and Durham, they had crisscrossed the state back and forth several times in the early days of her life. Her memories begin really in Durham, though, where her parents finally settled. Her father, Garland, was a cobbler and a fine finish carpenter, but he had a disease. It was not the kind that a doctor can cure but instead comes in the form of a bottle. He fought it for years, and he would get sober for a while, but it would always return. Her mother, Catherine, was a short, spark plug of a woman that loved him despite. More times than not, she had to shoulder the burden of mother and father as she tried her best to raise and care for her five children. It created a tough veneer that hid a tender heart for most of her life.

When Kathy first met Robert, she didn't pay him a lot of attention but to hear Robert tell it, he knew from the first moment he saw her in Mrs. Montgomery's fifth-grade class that one day she would be his wife. He would sometimes watch her from his porch as she pushed a cart down the street, collecting bottles to exchange for money. One afternoon through the screen door on the back of his house, Robert saw Kathy riding off on his bicycle. He gave chase but could not catch her. Robert breathlessly watched her go down the street as he stood stooped with his hands on his knees, breathing hard, helpless. He couldn't believe such an angel could steal his bike, but by nightfall, it had reappeared. Kathy would later deny the accusation of bicycle theft. Still, she would allow the caveat that if she did, she was "just borrowing it" and was plainly doing it to flirt with him. It was not until they were in high school that Robert really made his move. In her industrial arts class, Kathy would see him pass by the door kicking his leg backward like Curly from the Three Stooges. She would stifle a giggle and try to motion him away before she got in trouble.

One night at a friend's house, Robert was talking about Kathy non-stop, and his buddy told him he should just call her. So, he did. He asked her if she would like to go for a ride, and after an agonizing few seconds of silence, she said yes. It was the two of them together then after. They loved each other so very much and wanted to get married as soon as possible. Robert knew what the answer would be if he were to ask for permission from her parents for her hand in marriage, so he decided not to even ask. Although they knew they would be breaking tradition by not formally asking for her hand, they also did not want to elope. They were in love and wanted their wedding to be a holy event blessed by God from the very beginning.

Kathy broke the news to her parents, as did Robert. They were not asking but telling them that they had decided to be man and wife. In anticipation of their wedding day, Kathy set about sewing her own wedding dress. Soon after, Robert sat on the corner of his bed in his room, struggling to put on the rented tuxedo shoes. "Something was wrong," he thought as he held the shoes out in front of him, trying to find a size printed inside. Robert looked over on the bed at the tuxedo that looked about three sizes too small also. "What the heck can I do now, today is the day?" he muttered under his breath as he tossed the shoe into the corner. This is certainly not the best start to a marriage. Then he heard an odd sound.

Clop, clop, clop, clop.

He sat listening to the sound reverberate through the small mill house. It was coming towards him down the narrow hall.

Clop, clop, clop, clop.

The walls and floor of the little house were paper-thin, and you could hear everything said and done in it most days. The sound persisted until it grew louder and reached the door to his room. He sat staring at the door as the doorknob turned and the rusty hinges creaked. The door opened, and there stood his dad. Robert Sr. was a small man and stood in the doorway draped in a tuxedo that was at least three times too big for him.

"I think I got the wrong suit, Bud!" he said, taking a few steps forward in the huge shoes, clopping as he came. It was just the moment Robert Junior needed to calm his nerves, and they began swapping out shirts, shoes, pants, and jackets to get ready for the big day.

They drove to a little country church in Orange County under live oak trees and rolling green fields. Robert paced nervously in the backroom as he waited for the moment to come when he could take his place at the altar and wait for his bride. His dad came into the room and closed the door behind him.

"Robert Junior," he said in a somber tone. "I want to talk to you about something."

"Ok, daddy," he said nervously, wondering what it could be that his daddy could need to talk to him about right now that was so important.

"Son," he began, "If you don't want to go through with this. If this is too much for you to handle, then you can strike out of that door right there, right now. You cross that backfield and wait for me on Pleasant Green Church Road. I will go out there and tell everyone that there is not going to be a wedding, and we appreciate them coming out today. I will explain everything and then come and pick you up." Robert just stood looking at his dad and didn't know what to say. He looked at him with confusion. This was not helping his nerves. Then his dad stared at him right in his eyes as he had always seen his dad talk to other men.

"If you do go out there, Robert Junior, then I expect you to uphold those vows you are about to make. It is not a game. It is a serious business, and if you make those promises to God, you better keep them. If you walk out of this room to get married, then I expect you to do it like a man or just walk away." There was a moment of pregnant silence in the room, broken only by the faint sound of an organ beginning to play in the church.

"Do you understand?"

"I do," Robert Jr. said, and his dad nodded his head in approval, a tear forming in the corner of his eye. "Well," he said as he stepped to the side and motioned to the door, "Let's go get married."

Moments later there in front of friends, family, and teachers, Robert watched as Kathy came through the doors of the church. She was the most beautiful thing he had ever seen. As she came close to him, he reached out his hand for hers, and that moment as they stood holding hands, their lives became as one. They became man and wife and a few months later walked one after the other across the stage of Durham High School to receive their diplomas as the Class of 1973.

After graduation, they settled into the same life as had Robert's parents: millhouse, cotton mill job, and family on their mind. Robert and Kathy knew they wanted to have children, but they also knew they did not want anyone to think that they had gotten married because a surprise was on the way. They didn't have to wait long for a family. Little Bud was born in 1975 and enjoyed a pretty good run as an only child as his mom and dad fussed over him. A few years later, in 1979, they welcomed their baby girl Tracy who took some of Bud's attention but seemed to make the family complete.

In late 1980, Kathy lost her father. He had struggled and tried to beat the bottle but had finally lost his fight. As she stood holding Tracy, watching Bud struggle against her sister Cheryl's grasp as they walked to the front of the chapel for his funeral, she felt sick. She assumed it was from the heartbreak of losing her daddy, but little did she know that she was in for a surprise. Ricky was born in July 1981, and with the family finally complete, they settled into a routine. Go to work, go home, dinner, kids, TV, then again, the next day. They soon found themselves looking to break free from the lives that they had and find a new adventure.

Chapter 5

The red clay dirt road and white flint rocks bumped under the truck as it rolled down the hill to a new home and a new adventure. On the very outskirts of Durham County in North Carolina, the Jackson family was moving to the country. They were like any other family in the area. Nothing extraordinary; in fact, they were probably a little more Roseanne than Full House like their peers. They were firmly in that upper echelon of America's poverty class in the '80s and '90s. The kids looked out of the windows at the trees and fields on both sides of the truck as they moved closer to the cabin that Robert and Kathy had built from nothing with their bare hands. On their right driving down the road was a white two-story farmhouse where the Mortons lived, Mr. and Mrs. Morton and their daughter, nicknamed Tootsie. She had Down Syndrome and was a constant companion at her mother's side no matter where you saw her.

They had come to this place after much thought and consideration. Robert had looked around at Durham, the city that had always been his home, and saw many changes that made him concerned about raising the kids in town. Durham was a mill town, and he and his father, grandfather and his great-grandfather had worked at the cotton mill that was right across the street from their current home on Rutherford Street. His father and namesake had moved to the country years before and had several acres. The Scots-Irish blood that coursed through his veins called him to an adventure. He took out some loans and spent what savings he and Kathy had to build a little cabin on the backside of his father's property. They would spend many happy years here in this little cabin. It was small, and there was one room that served as the living room and bedrooms for the entire family and was heated by a cast-iron potbellied wood stove. The heat of the summer was held at bay by a window air conditioning unit.

Robert and Kathy were young parents on a mission to build a life there among the pine trees and oaks. When they moved to the country, "Little Bud," who was in actuality William Robert Jackson III, was an eight-year-old and already a little man. He was known to don his tan polyester leisure suit and, with his Gideon New Testament, stand atop a coffee table and deliver fiery sermons to anyone that would listen. Tracy was four and a blond bombshell if ever there was one. As Kathy and Robert had built the cabin from the ground up, she had run from tree to tree, giggling and playing.

Before moving in, construction of the cabin was tedious work. Ricky was little more than a baby. At times during the little cabin's construction in the woods, Kathy would have to abandon Robert to hold his own board, or he would have to tuck a flashlight under his chin for light so she could breastfeed the crying babe in the white bassinet.

Hard work and adventure had been just what they were looking for. As they moved in, they felt the satisfaction that most people never feel of genuinely creating something. The years in the little cabin were happy ones. Robert frequently hunted and fished while experimenting with ownership of livestock. One day he would show up with pigs, then maybe he would come home with a mule or a goat. Kathy always turned to and supported whatever he had going on. Surely expressing concern in private, but she was always there beside him building a pen or feeding the critters. The kids learned many lessons in the country that were not available in the city, catching crawdads and frogs among them. Hunting, fishing, and reading the woods came with time. Enjoying the morning sounds of birds singing and animals awakening from slumber is something not everyone gets to know. Some will never enjoy it, but once you do, it is like a drug that a person craves if they have gone without it too long.

One day the mill that had employed Robert and his father and back two more generations closed. Robert's dad decided to take his retirement money, buy a new Ford Escort, and drive to the Florida Keys. Pop and Granny spent time together that they had not had for decades and reflected on what their last stage in life would look like. They came home and settled down in the home they had made there in the woods. Robert Junior was close by with his kids, and although money would be tight, Pop and Granny figured they could make it.

Just a short few yards away from his parents' house, Robert Junior was not so sure. He looked at his situation much differently than his parents did. Robert Junior had three small children, and no leads for anything else. He knew he could not miss a paycheck and set out in his Chevy step side truck the next morning just as if he were going to work. Really, he was. Except now, his job was to find a job. A quarter in a newspaper machine and an ink pen were his tools. All-day long, he circled ads, made phone calls, and then crossed through ads. He came home that night feeling dejected and hurt. As he pulled his truck up in front of the cabin, he could see Kathy through the kitchen window. He turned the truck off and closed his eyes for a moment. He had never felt so low. What was a man who could not take care of his family? The side door burst open, and two small blonde heads appeared smiling at him. He sighed and forced a smile as he went inside to face them. The little ones had no idea what was going on, and even though Bud may have understood what had happened, Robert knew that he had no way of knowing how he was feeling. He scooped them up and bounded inside to find a hot meal and a smiling wife just as he always had.

They all slept in the big room—the boys on a bunk bed and Tracy on a small bed in the corner. Robert and Kathy had a mattress that they kept under the bunk bed and pulled out at night to sleep on. When they put the kids to bed and settled down, Robert found himself looking up at the ceiling with so many thoughts running through his mind. Emotions that he had not felt in many years began to surface and drove him from the bed and into the bathroom as if he were sick. Robert ran across the living room and into the bathroom as if he would throw up but instead, he shut the door behind him and began to sob. He sat on the side of the bathtub and, with his face in his hands, cried like he had not cried in so many years. Maybe ever.

How could he keep facing these kids, knowing he was not providing for them? What kind of father was he?

He looked up when he heard the door creaking and saw Kathy there in her nightgown.

"Robert," she whispered. "Are you ok?"

He felt even more ashamed than he had a second before and tried to stifle back the tears, but they seemed to come even stronger. Kathy crossed the room and wrapped her arms around him. His wife, who had always been right beside him as his partner in life, now seemed matronly. She comforted him as he opened up to her about how he was feeling. She listened to him and then sat down across from him on the toilet.

"Robert," she said. "You have no reason to be feeling the way you are feeling," she said. "You didn't have anything to do with the mill shutting down. You didn't lose your job because you were lazy or couldn't come to work on time. It just went away. It was just something bad that happened that we have to deal with. God wouldn't have put anything in front of us that we can't handle."

He was comforted by her as he looked into her blue eyes. He could see the strength that he had always admired. He could see what his children saw. He would never look at her the same way again.

"We don't know what God has in store for us, Robert," she continued. "You just need to get out there and figure out what it is. We are behind you."

Robert wiped his eyes and kissed her. He stood up from the side of the bathtub there in the cabin, more determined than he ever had been before to do what needed to be done. Although sleep alluded him, he was up again the next morning to get back at it. It was not long before things changed for them forever. One morning a few days later, he was walking out of the door to look for work when the phone rang. He was standing in the doorway, but something told him to stop. He turned and looked at the yellow phone hanging from the wall as it rang, and he just knew. He walked to it and picked it up.

"Hello."

"Hello, is this Robert Jackson?"

"Yes, ma'am."

"This is Nancy Williams at the North Carolina School of Science and Math. I was calling you back about the maintenance job you applied for."

He got the job and ended up not missing a paycheck. The job with the state was a blessing in more ways than one. Not only was he able to keep working, but he also found that he was making more and had better benefits. Another plus was that the retirement payout he received would not have to be spent to keep the kids fed; he could now use it to buy the two-story house on the top of the hill.

Recently, Mr. Morton had passed away, and Mrs. Morton and her daughter were moving out. The owner of the house that was renting it to them was looking to sell, and Robert had big dreams of fixing the place up and moving his family into a bigger home. He loved the idea of being in a larger place and still being close to his parents. So, Robert made an offer and soon found that he was now a homeowner. But he would find that long days and hard work were on the horizon like he had never experienced as he and Kathy tried to get the house ready to move their family into.

Chapter 6

The days became long for Robert and Kathy after purchasing the house. Robert worked all day, and as soon as he got off, he would go straight to work on the remodel. It was slow going working by himself. He had worked construction and considered himself a decent carpenter, but he was amazed at what he could accomplish on his own. Even lacking another person to hold a flashlight or a board in place had been a real challenge. Still, he had made it work and found himself collapsing in bed most nights for a few hours slumber until the alarm clock informed him of the coming of the next day's marathon of things to do. Many times, he did not even make it home, stopping at the top of the hill to go straight to work on the new house. Kathy would appear with a hot plate of food and the kids to visit, and then it was back to the grind.

Kathy was busy with the kids. She was in constant motion - dropping off, picking up, and cooking meals. She was a master at making it work and could take the barest ingredients and turn them into a meal fit for a king. Years later, her kids would swear that their mom had been the inspiration for the Food Network program Chopped, where chefs were given a basket of random ingredients and were expected to make a gourmet meal. They could picture their mom looking into the cabinets and refrigerator:

"Alright, three days till payday, and we have canned salmon, snap beans, and some candy leftover from Halloween. Let's go!" They were never disappointed. She seemed tireless, and in the evenings, to make extra money, she would settle down the kids and clean a local office building. She often stopped at the new house afterward and worked with Robert until they were both too exhausted to continue. The years after the mill shutdown would prove to be the busiest of their lives, but they faced them together every step of the way.

It was Kathy that first noticed odd energy about the house. She would get a chill many times while there or feel like someone was watching her. Robert would ask her to grab a tool, and it would not be where he said it was. At first, this was blamed on him just misplacing it. His mind was so wound up that he hardly thought of any other alternative than that or one of the kids walking off with it. Still, Kathy began to notice this would happen when she had just had something herself. Early on, it was nothing that would slow them down or give them pause, but it was enough for Kathy, for a brief moment at least, to stop and ponder what was going on. In these moments, though, she watched Robert as he charged on and kept her concerns to herself, being ever the loyal wife. She was a woman of "pioneer stock," as Robert would say. He never took a step in this world since they were kids without her close beside him.

Time passed, walls fell, and others went up in their place. Robert and Kathy tore the house down room by room and rebuilt it from the inside. Life was hectic, and the kids were growing. Bud was a constant help to Kathy and was often at her side, cleaning the office building at night or watching the little ones for her when she was gone. Most of the time, he tortured them relentlessly when she was gone, but nothing outside of his rights as the oldest. Ricky and Tracy played in the shadow of the old house that they would soon call home. Army men fought battles in the grass of the front yard, and mud pies were made in freshly dug holes that would one day be the foundation placed under the old house. Although busy and stressful times, they were also full of many good memories.

Once Robert was working on something, and Ricky, snot-nosed and teary-eyed, reported some transgression that Bud had committed against him. Robert was busy and just wanted to focus on his task. He looked over, and Bud was playing in the dirt with his Hot Wheels cars. He didn't look like he was doing anything that should be causing such a fuss.

"Alright, alright, just stay away from him then if he is bothering you," he said. Ricky sulked away, and Robert went back to work. It seemed like just a few minutes later when the little blonde head appeared again.

"Bud hit me!" he pleaded.

Robert, in frustration, said, "Well, just hit him over the head with a board! Then he will leave you alone."

Ricky once again left him to his work. He focused on what he was doing. Tongue out and sweat dripping onto his lap as he worked a new saw blade into his Skill saw; Robert became aware of a slight movement in his peripheral vision. He looked up and saw Bud still playing in the dirt with his cars, but Ricky caught his attention. Ricky was holding a 2x4 board that was longer than he was tall, over his head creeping up behind Bud. He was about to send Bud into orbit! Robert dropped what he was doing and ran towards Ricky waving his hands,

"Stop! Stop!" he yelled as he ran across the yard and took the board from Ricky. The crisis was averted, and a trip to the emergency room was avoided. Still, Robert realized that maybe he needed to watch his instructions to his youngest, who obviously took him very literally.

Some tools were stolen from the house one night, and it was a massive hit to Robert and Kathy. They went through the same feeling that anyone has when they are robbed. It is upsetting knowing that someone has taken something from you and violated your space. It was an ominous feeling that the house they would soon move their family into had been broken into, and a person or persons had walked in and out of the rooms where they would soon sleep searching for valuables. It was more than that, though; the tools that had been stolen were hard to replace. They were stretched about as thin as possible now, and the thought of having to find the money to replace the tools was daunting. They were in a pretty tight box, though. The house had to be finished because of the large investment they had put into it already, but they did not have the extra money for the tools. Creditors were already calling, and the wolf was at the door most of the time. It was only by the grace of God and Mastercard that got them through. Robert began to sleep nights in the house alone with his pistol to guard the new tools. This allowed him to work even later some nights, although it kept him from seeing Kathy and the kids just that much more.

On one of these nights, Robert was working in the bedroom where he and Kathy would call their own one day. It was late, and he was working on the sub-flooring bent over and concentrating. He was close to the wall where there had once stood a fireplace. The brick chimney was still there, but the inside of the fireplace had been closed up years before. When he had torn out the walls, he found the bricks and a small opening to the chimney, but he had plans to close this hole before installing the sheetrock and closing in the room. As he worked, he suddenly felt the hair on the back of his neck stand on end. He stopped working but stayed on his knees there on the floor. He could see the goosebumps appearing on his arms, and he could feel someone's eyes on him. He had never before so strongly felt that he was not alone when he was supposed to be. Robert was absolutely sure that someone was in the house with him and was watching him. He slowly laid down his hammer and reached to his side for his Ruger. He pulled it from his holster and turned to the doorway of the room as he cocked it and raised it to welcome anyone that had broken in once more.

What he found when his head turned was an empty doorway and a silent house. He was sitting upright now, pointing his pistol at an empty door. He felt silly, yet he still felt like he was being watched. He exhaled. He must just be tired, he thought. As he lowered his gun and turned back to his work, his eyes caught his stalker face to face. The round black eyes stared at him just a few feet away. A forked tongue shot out towards him, flicked, and then retreated back into the mouth of a snake that hung out of the brick chimney who had obviously had his sleep disturbed by the late-night construction. Robert again raised the pistol, and the snake drew back as if to strike. He gently squeezed the trigger, and the gun exploded to life in his hand. The snake dropped straight down into the chimney, dead. "Change of plan," Robert thought, "move closing the chimney to the top of the to-do list."

Chapter 7

As the renovation moved along, Robert ran into a problem that he had very little control over - the building inspector. He had worked construction and carpentry all of his life, and there was not much he couldn't do, but making something work and making something to code are two different things. Robert reached out to a buddy from work who was a licensed electrician named Lynwood Thompson. They worked on the house's final wiring and checked everything twice to make sure it was right for the inspector who was coming in the morning. It was summertime, and the days were long. Robert and Lynwood leaned on the hood of his truck after a long day, satisfied that everything was right and the inspection would go well the next day. They were both so tired that they found themselves talking for longer than they both had expected, and the last light of the summer day began to fade. Night crept around them, and although it was still light enough to see outside, it was dark enough to illuminate the upstairs window of the house where a work light had been hung up and left on.

As they talked, Lynwood said it was probably time for him to head home. He was standing by the door of his truck, and Robert leaned against the hood at the front. Robert agreed it had been a long day and they should head home, thanking him again for all of his help. Lynwood opened his door to leave and pointed to the upstairs window, "Your son is still here," he said. Robert turned and looked over his shoulder, seeing a boy's silhouette in the window, and nodded in agreement. He figured it must be Bud, and he would get him when he went up to turn the light out before he went home for the night. As Lynwood left, Robert told him that he was so excited for his family. They had never had things before like they would when they moved into the house. They had grown up in mill houses and the cabin, and even something as simple as having your own room was foreign to them. He wanted to get it done as soon as possible so they could enjoy these things, and he tried to make things as nice as possible for them. He saw the sacrifice that they all made every day. Kathy worked tirelessly with the kids, cleaning buildings and right along beside him as much as possible. Bud had to spend a lot of time watching the two younger kids, and Tracy and Ricky had to sacrifice the time spent with mom and dad while they were working so much. As Robert could see the end of the remodel, he could envision a bright future for his family.

They parted ways, and Robert watched the tail lights of Lynwood's truck disappear up the road. He turned and looked up at the window seeing only the light coming through an empty window space. He walked into the house and called out for Bud.

"Hey Bud, turn the light off up there, and let's head home." He got no response.

"Bud," he called again, but he got no answer.

He started up the stairs to the bedroom, seeing the light coming from the door as he crested the top of the stairs.

"Bud!" Nothing.

He pushed the door open and could see that the room was completely empty except for the light and a few small tools. He just couldn't imagine Bud taking off down through the woods at night without waiting for him or letting him know he was heading home. He searched all of the upstairs and downstairs. After Robert locked up the house, he walked around outside, calling for Bud, but he was nowhere to be found. Finally, he jumped in his old truck and made the short trip down the road to the cabin.

"Bud must have headed home by himself right after he saw him," he thought as he drove down the hill.

When he walked into the door of the cabin, Kathy was putting his dinner on a plate.

"Is Bud home?" he asked.

"Sure," she said, "He came home with me three hours ago."

Robert was taken aback. He asked if she was sure, and she said yes, he had been playing with Tracy and Ricky and watching TV all evening.

"That's strange," Robert said. He told her what had happened, and Kathy felt a tinge of trepidation run through her. She already felt a little funny about the house but had always shoved the feeling down and moved forward towards their dreams. Still, she thought that maybe he was mistaken and had just seen some other shadow that played a trick on them for a moment. Perhaps it was the position they were standing in, or maybe they were just tired. She tried to push any negative thoughts to the side, but she would soon get confirmation of her fears. She would face the reality that they were moving to the house, but they would not be the sole occupants.

Not long after Robert saw the boy in the window, Kathy would have her suspicions confirmed with a real and terrifying experience. Kathy was exhausted. She was busy with all of her usual tasks, and helping Robert as much as possible with the house. As the renovation neared its end, things got even busier as they rushed to complete the task and move on to the next stage in their young family's life. Kathy and Robert were working every spare minute on the house, and it was on one of these days right before they were set to move in when exhausted they lay down to rest on the floor in the living room. They lay together on the new carpet that had just been installed, and Robert wrapped his arms around her and pulled her close. They intended to just rest a moment and then get back to the finish work. A smile spread over her face as she looked around the room at their new home. It was no time until they had both fallen fast asleep.

When she awakened, she could tell the sun was retreating through the trees. The kids were with Robert's parents, so they were fine, but she knew she needed to wake Robert and finish up so she could go and make dinner. She could hear Robert slightly snoring in her ear, and his arm felt heavy against her. She suddenly became aware of a presence in the room. She was enveloped by an energy as if someone was smothering her. The rancid smell of body odor, dirt, and tobacco filled her nostrils as she lay unable to move or cry out. It was a smell she had smelled many times in her life, passing on the street or standing behind an old farmer that had been in the hot sun all day in the grocery store. It had never been this strong, though, and never this close. It was as if the smell was on top of her there on the floor. Her eyes were wide, and she gasped for air. Her mind raced with fear, and then suddenly, as quickly as the presence and the smell overtook her, it was gone.

She wiggled out from under Robert's arm and sat up, looking around. There in the first moments of dusk, she decided that she would keep the experience to herself, at least for now. Robert opened his eyes and smiled at her.

"I better get going and get dinner on," she said and left him there to finish up alone. She would have this experience again on more than one occasion on the stairs, hall, and living room. She would always keep it to herself until someone else shared their experience with the presence and the smell of an old farmer. That would not be for many years. For now, she was just focused on what was important, which was taking care of her family. In the cabin, she contemplated the experience but shook it off and rolled up her sleeves to feed the Jackson family.

Chapter 8

"A house is never still in darkness to those who listen intently; there is a whispering in distant chambers, an unearthly hand presses the snib of the window, the latch rises. Ghosts were created when the first man awoke in the night."

- J.M. Barrie

By 1990, the house was ready to move into. It had been a tough four years while they had done all of the renovations. Robert had replaced the creek rocks that once served as the foundation for the house by jacking up the house one corner at a time and laying the brick foundation. The whitewashed clapboard had been covered with white vinyl siding. The plaster walls on the interior had been replaced by sheetrock. The antiqued wiring of the house had been totally replaced. Carpet, flooring, and paint had been applied to all of the rooms. Entering the front door, the living room had remained the same size, but Robert had installed decorative tiles on the ceiling. There was a stained-glass window on the back wall at the foot of the staircase, which led to a landing where the door immediately across from the top of the stairs was Bud and Ricky's room. The door to the right was Tracy's room.

Downstairs, to the right of the living room, was Robert and Kathy's room, and straight to the back of the house was the kitchen. Robert had installed cabinets from the old Watt's hospital taken out to make way for more modern fixtures in the now growing North Carolina School of Science and Math (NCSSM). The kitchen had an open ceiling and had a chandelier hanging over the kitchen table. The wall that made up the kitchen's interior was shared by Robert and Kathy's room on the bottom and Bud and Ricky's room at the top. The back of the house had windows overlooking the backyard. When the foliage died in the winter, you could see the cabin where they lived and Granny and Pop's house. On the left side of the kitchen, where there was once a door leading out to the backyard, they built a bathroom and a back porch onto the house. The two outhouses that were on the property when they bought it had to be torn down to meet building code. It had been quite the transformation, and they were all excited to move into their new home.

They moved their belongings by hand up and down the hill on the path that would be worn and grow wider over the years. They had spent so much time together and had grown used to sleeping in the same room and sharing a small space. Robert and Kathy soon sensed the trepidation of the kids as night and bedtime approached. Ricky and Tracy had never had their own rooms before and had always slept near their parents. Bud had been the only kid that had known what it was like to have his own room when they lived in town, but he had been small and could barely remember it. Kathy thought that it would help if she did something special for the kids to ease their nerves a bit, so she decided to bake some of her peanut butter delight, which the kids loved. Ricky and Tracy sat with Robert in the living room and watched television while Kathy baked in the kitchen. Bud, getting older and more independent, could hardly wait to enjoy having his own space, even if he had to share it with his younger brother. He yawned and said he was going to bed.

Bud went up the stairs to his room and closed the door behind him, and sighed. It was so nice to be able to have some level of privacy. When he was in his room, the world went silent. No one could ever say Robert Jackson did not insulate the house. The television, laughter, and clanking of pots and pans in the kitchen went away with the closing of the door. He stepped over the collection of Hot Wheels and Micro Machines lined up on the floor by his bed where he had been looking at them earlier. They were in perfect lines on the blue carpet like a tiny car lot. He had always loved old cars. The metal and plastic replicas were his way of marveling at the different models and styles of American muscle cars. He closed the blinds and turned off the lights. Bud liked to sleep in the dark, which he rarely had been able to do the last few years, and an issue that would arise with his younger brother sharing the room with him.

Bud took his place on the bottom bunk and settled down for his first night in the house, enjoying the darkness and quiet he had missed for so long. Sleep came over him quickly, and he felt himself entering into that hazy land of being half asleep and half-awake when he was jolted back to the land of the conscience. Across the room, he heard something move. He pulled the blanket up around his neck and slowly opened his eyes, but they met only the darkness of the room. "Did he really hear something?" he thought.

The door was still closed, so he knew that Ricky had not come to bed, and if he had, he would be complaining about keeping the door opened, or he would be tossing and turning on the top bunk. Something annoying would be happening if Ricky was in the room, but he wasn't. Maybe he had fallen asleep briefly and dreamed he heard something, he thought. Then there in the darkness staring into the darkroom, he heard something again. This time it was distinctive and real. Footsteps came across the room towards him. Bud covered his head with the blanket and curled in a ball, turning towards the wall as the steps came towards him. He was paralyzed with fear, and although he wanted to call out, he could make no sound. If he did, he wondered if anyone would even hear him.

As the footsteps reached the side of his bed, Bud's paralysis was broken by the sound of Hot Wheels and Micro Machines scattered under the invisible footsteps of an intruder. He could hear them flying across the floor and hitting the wall. He began to feverishly beat the wall with his fists, hoping that someone would come for him.

It seemed an eternity, but downstairs in the kitchen, Kathy had heard the beating and immediately headed upstairs to see what in the world Bud was doing. She topped the stairs, turned the hall light on, and threw the door open to Bud's room.

"What in the world is going on in here!" she said angrily, thinking Bud wanted something and was just being too lazy to go down the stairs and get it himself.

Bud, whose courage was slowly returning with the arrival of his mom, peeked out from under the covers at her and then peered over the side of the bed to the floor. The cars were scattered all over the room! The realization that it had not been a dream swept over him, and he looked at Kathy who's anger subsided when she saw her oldest son's face.

"Bud, what happened?"

She turned on the light in the room and sat down on his bed as he told her what he had experienced. She did her best to keep him calm and assure him that there was nothing there in the house that could hurt him and that everything would be ok. Her mind raced back to the presence she had sensed and smelled not long ago. She calmed him down, and for once, Bud was happy to see the blonde hair of his tiny roommate coming up the stairs and bouncing up the ladder to the top bunk. He didn't complain about the door being left open that first night.

Kathy went back to the kitchen and put the peanut butter delight in the refrigerator to firm up and began to clean up. She was worried about the strange occurrences, and now whatever it was, had begun to affect the kids. Bud's first night in the house was not the most restful night he would spend in the house. She lay awake beside Robert as he slept, listening to the quiet of the night around her, listening for the banging on the wall that after that day would become a signal from the boys that something was going on upstairs.

She didn't hear it again that night, but she would hear it again soon.

Chapter 9

The night was pierced by a high-pitched, blood-curdling scream that reverberated throughout the house. It awakened everyone in the house. Robert opened his eyes and thought, "Was that a dream?" In the dim moonlight flooding into the bedroom from the window, he could see the outline of Kathy next to him. When he saw her sit up, he thought, "If it is a dream, then Kathy is having the same one." He sat up in bed, and she turned to him.

"Did you hear the…….." she asked, but before she could finish, another scream severed her words, and Robert was out of bed. Leaping over her with a bound, he disappeared through the door. It was unmistakable, the scream was coming from upstairs, and Kathy bounced out of bed right on his heels. It had been years since they had moved so fast, and within seconds, they were running up the stairs three at a time. Robert could see Bud in the doorway of his room with Ricky peering out from behind him. They had heard it too, and he could see the fear and confusion on their young faces. He turned to Tracy's door at the top of the landing, which was still closed, and laid his shoulder into it. He was going through that door whether his hand was able to work fast enough to turn the handle, or he broke it down. Tracy needed her daddy, and he was there.

The door flung open, and in a single motion, Robert hit the light switch and crossed her bedroom to the far side of the room where her bed was. Kathy was right behind him, and Bud and Ricky followed her. The entire family had come to her aid. As soon as the light came on and Tracy saw her daddy, she sat up on the side of her bed. They could all see that she was hysterical and crying. Her face was red, and tears streamed down her face. Her chest heaved, and she could hardly breathe. The family could also see that she was alone in the room. Robert stopped short of the bed and let Kathy overtake him. This looked like a job for a comforting mama bear and not a snarling and vicious papa bear coming to the defense of his cub. He stepped back to where the boys were standing, and they watched as Kathy sat beside Tracy and comforted her by holding her close and rubbing her sweat-soaked hair. Some women just take to being a mother seamlessly, and Kathy had been one of those women. Robert knew that she would make it all better.

As Kathy sat with her on the bed consoling her, Bud noticed something odd. Tracy's bed had no blanket or sheet on it. He stared at the bare bed where Tracy and his mother sat and then looked at his dad. Robert had an odd look on his face also as he had noticed the same thing. He scanned the room, and Bud followed his gaze. Behind them, near the door and across the room from Tracy's bed, was an old Victorian modeled dollhouse that Robert had made for her. They had run right past it as they came into the room but now Robert, Bud, and Ricky were staring back at it as Kathy calmed Tracy down. The dollhouse was there but over the top of it were the blanket and sheet from Tracy's bed. It was draped perfectly over the dollhouse as if it had been held over the top of it by two people and dropped. It was such an odd sight that they just stood transfixed on it until they were jolted out of their trance by Kathy.

"Can you tell me what happened?" she asked. Robert and the boys turned back to Kathy and Tracy as she sniffled once more and began her story.

She said that she had been woken up and realized that she was cold. Still half asleep and with closed eyes, she reached out for her covers but could not find them. She thought she must have kicked them to the bottom of her bed or even off the side of the bed, so she opened her eyes and sat up to find them. Her blinds were opened, and the moonlight illuminated her room enough for her to see a woman sitting on the side of her bed in a white nightgown. Tracy rubbed her eyes and said, "Mama." When Tracy spoke, the woman turned her head, and her eyes and Tracy's met. There in the moonlight, Tracy could see that this woman was not her mama at all. She peered into the eyes of a total stranger, and the woman looked back at her, totally expressionless. Tracy put her hands over her eyes, curled up, and began to scream until she heard her door burst open.

Robert made a walk over to the closet and looked inside and then under the bed, more to make Tracy feel safe than to find an intruder.

"There is nobody here, baby," he said to Tracy to beguile her.

He looked at Kathy, whose eyes were fixed on the dollhouse. She pulled Tracy closer, and she began to sob again. Kathy looked over at Robert with a knowing gaze. She knew that no physical woman could have been in the room with her. The boys met them at the top of the stairs, and they would have seen her pass them going down the stairs, or the woman would have had to go into their room to miss Robert and her on the stairs. The blanket and sheet over the dollhouse told her it was not just a dream. Tracy would have had to pull the blanket and sheet off and then tossed them over the large dollhouse and spent the time adjusting and pulling it straight to make it look like it was now.

"Everything is alright," Kathy said, "You boys get back to bed."

"Listen to your mama," Robert said as he walked behind the boys and shut the door. Kathy laid Tracy down, and she and Robert got the sheet and blanket off of the dollhouse and draped it over her. Kathy tucked it in and made sure Tracy was snuggled in the warm blanket. Robert walked around the dollhouse, looking at it as if some clue would be found, or there may be some ghost fingerprints visible.

"You go on back to bed, daddy," Kathy said as she lay down beside Tracy and pulled her close. "I am going to lay with her awhile." Robert went to Tracy's bed and kissed both of them on the head. Then he peeked into the boys' room, where they were in bed with the lights off but were talking through the crack between the top bunk and the wall. He told them to go on to sleep, and he went back down the stairs. Never really able to sleep without Kathy in bed with him, he lay awake the rest of the night looking at the ceiling in the pale light of the moon. Kathy lay awake too beside Tracy as she cried herself to sleep in her mama's arms.

Chapter 10

Months and seasons passed for the Jackson family, and they settled into the house. Odd little things happened, and they all became aware of the presence. It was mostly little occurrences that would be an inconvenience like something going missing or a bump here or there in the house became a part of life for them all. One of the things that they seemed to "lose" most often was a pair of Kathy's sewing scissors. She had learned to sew in high school and continued to use this skill over the years. Halloween costumes, stuffed animals, and repaired garments flowed through her sewing machine. The scissors were large with a pink plastic handle and blades that came out from the handle at an angle and then flattened out, allowing Kathy to run them flat on a surface and cut fabric in a straight line. These scissors were not just for sewing, though, and were used for everything. Opening boxes, cutting off tags, and doing school projects were constantly on the agenda for the scissors, which were often used. Kathy had insisted that they be kept in the small drawer at the end of the counter, and when they were used, they had to be put back immediately.

Much to her annoyance, this rarely happened as smoothly as she would have asked for it to, and many times she would find that someone would use them and not put them back in the drawer. She would get so mad and have a speech, or worse, ready for whoever had them last. Strangely though, the scissors started to go missing with nobody claiming responsibility for taking them. Kathy found this very odd because everyone in the family had always been honest about these types of things. Even at the risk of being in trouble, the kids would always tell her the truth when questioned, so she thought that maybe someone had taken them and just forgotten. Then, the oddest thing would happen. Someone would find the scissors in the refrigerator right on the top shelf. This happened over and over in the first few years they lived in the house and was just one of the small things they will never forget.

Years passed, and Robert had moved from the maintenance department at NCSSM to the security department. He had a crazy schedule of seven days on and seven days off, alternating between day shift and night shift. The schedule really kept his sleep schedule in chaos. It seemed that as soon as he would get used to sleeping during the day and working all night, it would change, and he would have to try to sleep at night so he could work during the day. Kathy also got a job at NCSSM as a receptionist with the special programs and research department.

Bud was nearing the end of his time as one of the Jackson children and stood on the precipice of adulthood. He was seventeen and just waiting for the time to pass until he could go into the military. He had met a spitfire of a Florida girl named Michelle at his job at Phar-Mor drug store, and they had become engaged soon after. After much wrangling by Robert and Michelle, Bud had opted to join the Coast Guard instead of the Marine Corps, a decision he would regret the first time the buoy tender pulled away from the dock, and he felt his insides bubble up to his mouth. One of his Chiefs would later tell Robert that he quickly learned to make sure he never got in between Bud and the rail. Because Bud was working mostly night shifts and Robert was working the security schedule, they spent many days at home together while everyone else was at work or school.

On one of these days, Bud and Robert were sitting in the living room watching television and talking. Robert was enjoying this time because he knew that his relationship with Bud was changing. He remembered when he was a young man and was also looking to marry young and start out into the world. Like any good father, he was filled with worry and excitement for Bud, and he truly loved Michelle, who he knew would be a great wife and partner for Bud. He knew they would make it, but he also knew there would be rocky days ahead for them, and he would be able to do little but watch. Robert felt closer to his own dad during this time because Pop knew exactly how Robert was feeling. As the Cartwrights wrapped up another adventure and the familiar closing theme of Bonanza played, Robert looked over at Bud.

"I'm getting hungry; how about you?"

Bud agreed, and Robert went into the kitchen to heat up a can of Dinty Moore beef stew on the stove. Bud could hear the electric can opener and then Robert emptying the contents of the can into a pot on the stove. The Bonanza theme struck up again on the television screen, and as the map of the Ponderosa burned, the telephone rang.

"I'll get it," Bud called, not wanting to delay lunch and knowing it was probably for him. He crossed the living room to Robert and Kathy's room, where the phone was. In the early days of cordless phones, the Jackson family was still tied to a phone tethered to the base by a spiral cord. This was a technology that no one in 1992 could have guessed would be as antiquated as butter churn in just a few years. Bud was right, and the call was for him. He sat on the side of his parents' bed and talked on the phone while Robert moved around in the kitchen, finishing up lunch. Bud looked out of the open window across the room and watched a squirrel bound across the driveway. Suddenly behind him through the open door of his parents' bedroom, he heard a metal spoon drop on the stove and bounce onto the floor.

"Did you see him?" Robert yelled from the kitchen. Bud turned and saw nothing but told his friend he had to go and raced the few yards out of the door and into the small hall where he could see his dad.

Robert was excited, maybe even scared, but it had all happened so fast and was such a shock he really didn't know how to feel at the moment. Seeing him like that unnerved Bud, who though almost grown himself, still looked at his dad as the rock of the family. If his dad was scared, Bud felt that by default, he must be scared too, even if he had no idea what had scared him.

"Daddy, what did you see?" he asked.

Robert took a few steps back and leaned against the kitchen counter. "You didn't see anything?" he asked again. Bud shook his head no. Robert took a breath and told him what had happened.

He was standing by the stove, giving the stew a last stir or two before taking it up, when something caught his attention. He looked up, and just a few feet from him in the doorway of the short hallway between the living room and the kitchen, he saw a gray form of a man coming from the direction of the bedroom where Bud was. The figure was walking across the kitchen to the wall on the far side of the room. It had to have been right where Bud was, he insisted.

"It came from right where you were sitting. I don't know how you could have missed it," Robert said.

"I was looking out of the window, and I guess it was behind me," Bud said as the hairs on the back of his neck stood on end.

Robert continued to describe the figure. He could tell it was a man, but it had no features. It was just a solid gray form that was transparent. He could clearly see the form, but he could also see right through it. The other thing about the figure that stood out to him was the way it moved. It was not floating or moving like a real person, but moving in a jerking motion like you would see someone move in one of the old Charlie Chaplin movies from the days when the camera could not keep up with the actors' movement.

Robert took his hat off and ran his hand through his hair. Bud did not know what to say but just stood there in the kitchen with his dad as he tried to collect himself. Robert looked past him at the wall where the figure had disappeared, and something hit him. He realized that where the figure had gone through the wall was where the backdoor of the house had been before he closed it in to add the bathroom, hallway, and back porch on the house. It seemed that the previous residents preferred the old layout to the new. This was the second time that Robert had seen an apparition in the house, and the first time he had been scared by it. When he saw the figure in the window upstairs during the renovation, he was sure it was Bud. Still, there was no mistaking what he saw just then, and the implications were undeniable. He had moved his family into a haunted house for sure. As they ate lunch, they talked about it, and the fear subsided. Whatever he had seen had not hurt anyone, although he was sure it had given his heart a good jolt.

Chapter 11

Bud and Michelle got married in October of 1993 and moved into the cabin that Robert and Kathy had built. They wouldn't be there long because Bud was scheduled to leave for Cape May, New Jersey for Coast Guard basic training in November. It was a huge event for the family. They had never been parted before and were close. When Bud married Michelle, it had truly been the gain of a daughter and not the loss of a son. Even when they were dating, they were always there with the family, and when they got engaged, Michelle lived with them for a few months sleeping in Tracy's room with her for a while when her mother moved to South Carolina. Bud going into the military signaled a fissure that they had never felt before. It was an unsure time for everyone, especially Bud and Michelle, because they had no idea where he would end up being stationed. He knew he could be as close as North Carolina or as far as Hawaii or Alaska. When Bud last spoke to his recruiter he told him to report to the MEPS station in Raleigh where he would have to stay in a hotel room with another recruit until the early morning when a bus would take them on their journey to Cape May. Bud sheepishly asked if he could stay at home one more night. Durham was not too far, and he promised he would not be late reporting in the morning. The recruiter made him promise he would not be late and made it clear that it would be a horrible start to his military experience if he showed up late, but he could also see that Bud was serious about his commitment and he would be there when he was supposed to be there so he agreed to let him go home.

Later that night, Robert and Ricky walked down the hill to say goodbye to Bud before he went to bed. They could see the side porch light through the trees as they descended the hill and Bud came outside to meet them. Robert walked up to his son and looked him in the eyes, the same little baby that made him a daddy so long ago. He had held him crying, taken him fishing, taught him how to ride a bike, and now he was a man standing in front of him. The thought flooded through Robert's mind how he had started off fatherhood with a lie. When they handed his son to him so many years ago, he had held him and looked at him in those same eyes that stared back at him now. He had looked into those eyes and made him a promise, "I will always be there for you," he had said. It was a lie, but an honest lie if there ever was such a thing. Robert had always tried to be there, but he had found that he could not always be there for his kids.

They had to venture out on their own, and now Bud was really going to be on his own. Sadness and pride ran through Robert's body, and when he opened his mouth to speak, he found that only a sob came out of his mouth. He began to heave and cry and wrapped his hands around Bud as if he were holding onto him with all of his might. He could feel Bud's hand patting his back as he cried. Ricky backed into the darkness, not wanting anyone to see him cry. He sat on a fallen tree and sobbed along with the other Jackson men that night. As Michelle drove Bud to MEPS a few hours later, Robert, Kathy, Tracy, and Ricky stood in front of the house as they passed by. Crying and waving, they said goodbye.

They burned a light in the window every night for Bud while he was gone, and everyone was excited when they found out that he was going to be stationed on a buoy tender based in Atlantic Beach at Base Fort Macon. This was just a few hours away, so they would be able to see them often, and the family settled into a new routine. It looked the same as before. Everyone was still working and going to school, but it was still different somehow. The family had to adjust to Bud being gone, and the Jackson five had become the Jackson four. The house seemed a little emptier without Bud and Michelle around, and although he had been aware of the presence in the house, the Jackson's youngest son was about to get a surprising initiation into the paranormal.

Chapter 12

"The only thing that stays the same is
Everything changes, everything changes."

"Time Marches On" by Tracy Lawrence

"Lock the door!!!"

Robert's voice rang out through the house from wherever he was to whoever was coming in the door, either front or back. They had moved to the country, but security was still critical to him. It was probably his Scots-Irish blood, but he was a stickler for making sure everything was locked up at all times. Being secure and protecting his possessions and territory was born into his blood and had been a trait of his ancestors. Both the front and back doors were items of pride for Robert. When renovating the house, he had thrown out the flimsy wood paneled doors with cracked lead paint and replaced them with beautifully carved wooden doors that had stained glass in them. The door mechanism consisted of a handle to open and close the door and a bolt lock. Locking the door required pulling the door closed and then manually locking the bolt.

One day Ricky was coming into the backdoor from Granny and Pop's house. He went there every day after school to watch Atlanta Braves games with Pop or *The Young and the Restless* with Granny. He knew he could always count on a peanut butter and jelly sandwich and a tall glass of milk made by Granny. Sometimes, if, for some reason, Granny was not there, then Pop would make him the sandwich and get him the milk in her place. It wasn't the same, but he always thought it was sweet that Pop wanted to do that for him. Pop probably watched them together at the kitchen table every afternoon and wanted to be a part of their tradition.

On one particular afternoon, Granny had been home and whipped up a fantastic PB and J as usual. Ricky was in a great mood as he bounded up the hill in great strides. He took the back steps in one great leap and busted through the backdoor. Ricky pulled the door shut with his right hand and took about two steps down the back hallway. He stopped dead in his tracks because he knew where he had messed up, and he knew what was coming. Ricky could hear the TV in the living room. "Daddy was up!" he thought. He had worked the night before, but now he was awake, and Ricky knew what he was coming.

"Lock the door!" Robert yelled from the couch in the living room.

Ricky did an about-face and reached out his hand to grab the lock, but his hand stopped in mid-motion, and he stared at the door in real amazement. The door was locked already.

"Lock the door!" Daddy yelled again.

He stood staring at the door running through in his mind how it could have been locked. There was no way; he had just come through the door. He had only touched it with one hand. He had opened it with his right hand and closed it with the same hand. Could he have done it and just forgotten that quick? He couldn't have done it without even looking at the door behind him.

"Yes, sir," he answered.

He reached out for the door and unlocked it. When the bolt passed the door frame, the door popped out just a bit. He tried to slide the bolt back into place, but he couldn't. The door had to be pushed in a little to line the bolt up with the frame, so it had to be done with two hands. He shook his head, not scared at all, just perplexed. He secured the door and walked around the corner to find his dad standing guard over afternoon TV in his underwear on the couch. Ricky took his place beside him as the young prince of the castle, and they watched as poor souls pummeled each other with chairs and a studio audience chanted, "Jerry, Jerry, Jerry."

On the rare occasion that Ricky went straight home after school, instead of going to see Granny and Pop, he would play either inside or outside with his army men. He had a pretty good collection that had been passed down from Bud to him. They were small military figures from many different historical armies throughout history. These were not the average green and tan army men that you get at the store. You see, their knowledge of history and of warfare was just much too sophisticated for green and tan soldiers. Bud and Ricky bought theirs from the hobby store after much saving and squirreling away of birthday money. They were about a quarter of the size of the green and tan army men that most kids play with, but they were very detailed and accurate. They had Yankees, Confederates, French Foreign Legionnaires, Zulus,

American Indians, Vikings, you name it, they had it. They were kept in a bucket that had once held Christmas cookies that had been long since eaten.

Whenever Ricky wanted to play, he would decide who the combatants were to be. He would then pour the men out and separate his opposing armies by hand. The best spot was at the landing at the top of the stairs between his and Tracy's room. The stairs to the second story were long and narrow wooden stairs at the back of the house. Narrow and dark, they were easily tripped on. One of the kids, or even Kathy or Robert, would often ride down the stairs on their bottom instead of walking down them on their feet. The door to Tracy's room was to the right, and straight ahead was the entrance to Ricky's room. It was about a four-by-six-foot area that was generally a clear level playing field aside from a small bookcase. Plus, it being hardwood and not carpet, it was perfect for supporting the army men who were easier to line up and move around without them tipping over due to the flat base the men stood upon.

One rainy afternoon Ricky came home and went straight to playing war on the landing. Tracy was older, and she was in the stage where she was often doing something after school with friends. Robert and Kathy were working, so he was a true "latch key kid" when his dad was on day shift. Ricky had gotten off of the bus and walked down that long country road that led to the house and had let himself in with a key he kept on a Duke Blue Devils keychain that his Aunt had given him for Christmas one year. Eager to get started on the battle he had been envisioning all day in his head, he headed straight for his room to get set up. It was just him and his army, and they were all geared up for a fight.

Ricky poured out and separated his armies in his room because the men were harder to stand up on the carpet, but easier to gather and put the ones that didn't make the cut back into the cookie bucket. He transported his men out onto the landing and began to place them in lines facing each other. Tracy's door was closed as per her strict instructions of never touching anything that she was attached to in any way under penalty of death.

He could not be sure who fired the first shot, but his armies began to do battle. Rifle and cannon fire engulfed the small space, and gun smoke rose above the tiny armies. The little soldiers struggled over green meadows, and the battle ebbed and flowed back and forth. Cannons blasted cavalry units, and men fell all over the field. Horses and men screamed in pain as smoke blocked out the sun. As the battle reached a fevered pitch, Ricky was torn away from his daydreaming and became conscious of a noise. It was a knocking noise that sounded far away. He wasn't sure where it was coming from or when it had started because it was so slight. Maybe it had been going on for some time, but he just hadn't noticed it. But now that he had heard it, he focused on it. He stopped playing and returned to the reality of his surroundings and listened as the noise grew slightly louder—just a knocking sound.

Knock...knock...knock...

He closed his eyes and tried to focus on the sound. It began to get louder and louder as the seconds ticked by. Suddenly he heard a loud bang that rattled him and opened his eyes. The first bang was followed by a series of louder hits that were close to him. His eyes followed the sound across the hall to the door of Tracy's room, where the noise was now most definitely coming from.

Bang...Bang...Bang...

He looked with disbelief at the door. The next bang he heard shook the door, and he jumped back. His eyes were transfixed on it as it began to shake with each additional boom. They were becoming more and more rapid in their cadence like there was someone on the other side of the door trying to get out, shaking with each blow from the inside! Sitting among his plastic army men, all of the courage and zeal that he had felt as he led his men into combat was fading fast. He was supposed to be the fearless leader, but instead, he sat on wooden legs with frozen blood, watching the door move violently in its frame. Suddenly he jolted back into reality with the thought... "I'm alone in the house." This was no prank on little brother!

Feeling that discretion is the better part of valor, Ricky got on his horse and rode off that battlefield as quickly as his little legs could carry him. Suddenly, all that was frozen was alive with energy. Down the stairs, he flew through the living room, through the kitchen, the back hall, and out the backdoor. He ran down the hill to the safety of Granny and Pop's house, stopping for a few moments behind their home to catch his breath. He looked back over his shoulder at the house as his heart pounded inside his chest. He knew that if he were to tell Granny and Pop what had happened, they would believe him, but he decided to keep it to himself. When his breathing calmed, and he was unable to hear his own heartbeat, he went around front and knocked on the door. Granny was tickled to see him and went to work, making him a sandwich and getting him some milk while he sat in her chair and watched Greg Maddox throwing heat at the New York Mets.

Ricky watched the clock and waited until he knew his mama would be home. At about 5:30, he hugged his grandparents and ventured back up the hill to the house. Ricky could see the van in the driveway and knew she was already home. Ricky came into the house the same way he had left through the back door. Kathy was already wide-open, making dinner and asked if he had heard from Tracy. He had not been home, he told her but did not elaborate. "Ok," she said with a sigh. Tracking her down was going to be one more thing on her list before she would be able to relax, which like most days, was about an hour after she had fallen asleep. Ricky crept through the living room and peeked up the stairs. He could see the light on in the hall at the top of the stairs, and everything looked normal. Ricky tiptoed up the stairs one at a time. His soldiers were in the same place he had left them. The door to his room was opened, and the door to Tracy's room was shut just like when he had fled the house.

He didn't have the courage to open the door to Tracy's room, but he hung around his room and waited. When Tracy finally came home, he pressed his ear against his door and listened as she walked up the stairs and into her room. No screams, no sounds of her being assaulted by anything demonic or supernatural. Whatever had been in there must have fled in the face of the real danger in the house, which was the heightened emotional state of a teenage girl.

Chapter 13

Puberty and teenage angst descended upon the Jackson house in the years after Bud left home. Tracy, who had been a daddy's girl her whole life, suddenly found herself at odds with everything Robert said or did. To her credit, she is not the only teenage girl to go through this experience. Still, it was definitely a significant event for the family because they had never had any strife among themselves. They had experienced much hardship, but they had faced everything as a family. Kathy found herself in the middle between her husband and daughter frequently. She struggled to illustrate to each of them how bull-headed they were and how they were not getting along because they were alike, not because they were different.

Several years passed in the little white house where the relationship between father and daughter was strained. The communication between them seemed to be either icy cold silence or fiery clashes. Neither of the two would take a step back or compromise their position. Kathy and Ricky often found themselves in the middle of these squabbles, and lines became drawn at times. Mostly it was Kathy desperately trying to find some middle ground, or sometimes just defending Tracy out of sheer motherly love, even if she was wrong. Although a natural instinct, it caused a great deal of discord between Robert and Kathy for a while. Ricky delighted in getting involved in the fights. He was at the age where he knew enough to keep up with what was going on but was kind of annoying about it at the same time. He was directly in the middle of the awkward age, and his presence at times would be enough to make Tracy scoff in disgust.

One night during this time, when Robert had just come off of working night shifts, he was up late watching TV. It was difficult for him to regain a regular sleep pattern for a few days after completing a seven-day stretch of overnights, so often he was awake while everyone else slept. Robert would often find his livid teenaged daughter coming down the stairs to berate him about the volume of the TV and how he was keeping her awake. So, when he heard her door open and footsteps coming down the stairs, he braced for the worst. When she appeared on the stairs in a white nightgown, she seemed to not even see him. He was pretty sure she was ignoring him on purpose because of some transgression he had committed, but he could not be sure. "Hey, Trace!" he said enthusiastically. He figured he would either get a smile or get cursed out. Either way, he was looking for a response. She walked past him and disappeared into the kitchen. She was on the way to the bathroom, he guessed.

He sat watching TV, thinking of how he could get a reaction from Tracy as she walked by. Truth is, he missed his little girl, but he was unwilling to just go along with whatever she wanted to do, whether it was right or wrong, just to get along. He loved her enough to tell her when she was doing wrong, and he stood by that. As he sat there, though, he noticed the time kept passing by, and Tracy was still in the bathroom. "Was she sick?" he wondered. Maybe Tracy was sleepwalking? She had been known to sleepwalk on occasion when she was smaller, but it had been a while. He decided he better go and check on her as it must have been at least half an hour since she had passed him. When the next commercial break started, he heaved himself out of his comfy spot and headed through the kitchen towards the bathroom. As he came closer, he noticed the door was opened, and the light was off. "Tracy," he said, but there was no response.

As he came to the door, he turned the light on and found that it was empty. Maybe he had fallen asleep after Tracy walked by, he thought. He turned off the light and headed back to the living room, and as quietly as he could, he walked up the stairs. Robert flipped on the light in the hallway between the kids' room and slowly turned the doorknob to Tracy's room. As the light from the hall lit up her room, he could see Tracy sleeping soundly in her bed. Robert must have fallen asleep after she went by, but he really didn't feel like he had. He had almost convinced himself of this when he noticed that she was sleeping in an old t-shirt and not a nightgown. He pulled the door closed gently and went back downstairs. He sat back on the couch and thought about what had happened. He was sure he had not fallen asleep, and he was sure Tracy walked by. "I have to start getting more sleep," he said to himself, and he turned the tv off and went to bed. More than being frightened by what had happened, he went to sleep that night with a heavy heart because, above anything else, he missed his little girl, and the way things were absolutely broke his heart.

Chapter 14

Life had progressed at a rapid pace for Bud since he had been seventeen. Within a year, he had gotten engaged, married, joined the Coast Guard, and moved away from home. He had almost become accustomed to the paranormal activity that took place back home. Still, it was on a ship a thousand miles from home when he became convinced that the ghosts were not tied to the farmhouse in Durham but could be anywhere.

In August of 1994, while serving onboard the Coast Guard Cutter Gentian in support of Operation Uphold Democracy, Bud was serving as a Fireman Apprentice. Since he had first come aboard, he had found that the low man on the totem pole had to hold up their end and some. Bud found himself standing watches overnight on the old ship in the hot, oily, and incredibly loud engine room. Even in the dead of night, he would sometimes check the temperature and find that it was 130 degrees or more. The watches were brutal. Day in and day out, he would stand watch as they patrolled the Caribbean enforcing the embargo President Clinton had levied on the dictator-controlled Hattian regime. Working his job and standing watch generally made for a sixteen-hour day for him every day.

On one of these hot nights at around 3:40 am, when he was relieved, he looked down at the watch on his sweaty arm and tried to decide what he should do. It was so early that no one was awake yet on the ship except those on watch or on the bridge. All of the lower decks were dead silent except for the engine room, where the engine's roaring sound drowned out everything else. The early rising cooks wouldn't be up for another thirty minutes or so, and he wanted to grab something to eat before he tried to get a little sleep.

He opened the hatch to leave the engine room, and closed it behind himself. The door drowned out the noise of the engines, and the long passageway stood before him. The red lights lit the passageway except for the log office. This was the only door along the corridor, and there was only one way in and one way out to the office. He could see the profile of his Chief standing in the doorway to the log office with the fluorescent light buzzing inside, casting his dark shadow into the dimly red-lit passageway. Bud turned and took off his earplugs and hung them up on the door. He thought it was a stroke of luck as he had needed to speak to him anyway and now would not have to get up earlier than he was already planning to track him down before his work shift started.

As he neared the door, the dark figure stepped back inside the room and slammed the door.

"That was strange," he thought as he continued to move towards the door. He was suddenly wondering if now was a bad time to bother the Chief, but he really needed to talk to him. As he reached the door, he took the handle with one hand, knocked three times, and turned the knob. Locked!

"Chief," he called through the shut door and knocked again. Nothing. "Here we go," he thought. The military is notorious for pranks, and he had found it accurate, especially for a new guy. He ran his hand in his pocket, retrieved his key, and opened the door. The room was small, and the light was out. He stood in the doorway looking into the room, waiting for the Chief to jump out at him, but there was nothing. He reached in and switched on the light to find the office empty. He looked behind the door and under the desk. "What in the world," he thought. There is one way in and one way out of the office, and he saw the door open, and he saw the Chief there. He backed out of the room and turned the light off as he went.

Confused but exhausted, he went back to his bunk and tried to get a few hours of sleep before work started. When he went back on duty, he found the Chief there and asked him about the incident that morning. The Chief told Bud that he had never left his berthing area that morning until it was time for his work to start. It really sunk in what had happened when he spoke to the Chief, and he was never entirely comfortable on the ship again, either in port or at sea. Bud only told the story a few times, mostly to other guys that worked the engine room. One night after he had been on the ship for a couple of years and was nearing the end of his time on board, he found a group of young sailors who had just reported aboard ship. Bud found them sitting together in the rec area and decided to give them a little scare. He sat down, and they gathered around to listen to the once like them new guy, but now the salty experienced sailor.

Bud told them his story, and their eyes widened as he concluded his tale. The look on their face was priceless, and Bud leaned back in satisfaction as they hung on his every word. As he finished, suddenly, the television hanging on the wall behind him turned off, and the papers on a corkboard beside the sailors flew up as if a great wind had rushed through the room. They looked back and forth at each other and then back at Bud as if he had somehow added special effects to his story. He was more surprised than they were, and now his eyes were wide. He knew that they were far below deck and that there was no way for a gust of wind to reach the room they were in. As they dispersed for the night, he was glad that he was leaving the ship and spent the next few years on base until he got out of the service and started a new chapter.

Chapter 15

Tracy seemed to follow the Rebel Without a Cause philosophy - the "What are you rebelling against?", "What do you got?" philosophy. She and Robert butted heads relentlessly, with Kathy often finding herself in the middle of the two. The harder Robert pushed against her rebellion, the harder she pushed back, leading to many bad decisions that resulted in tumultuous teenage years and a difficult start to her adult life. One weekend when Robert and Kathy had driven to the coast to visit Bud and Michelle, they received news that broke their hearts. Bud had been waiting for his parents to arrive when his phone rang. It was Tracy, and she was sobbing. He calmed her down and asked what was wrong. "I'm pregnant," was her reply. "Could you tell mama and daddy for me?" she asked, saying that she was too scared to. It was not a duty Bud wanted, but he was her big brother, and he felt obliged to help her. He told them over dinner and watched the sadness and concern spread over their faces.

Tracy left home as not much more than a child herself. She headed into a cruel world, in trouble and scared but determined to start a family, albeit prematurely. She married her boyfriend and moved into the cabin that Robert and Kathy had built. It was a rocky time and although all prayed for a happy ending, what life doled out was far from it. Tracy delivered a son prematurely named Christopher, but he passed away hours after he was born. Her marriage ended soon after, and she moved back home. She found that it was impossible to go back even to the way things were before and soon moved out again. The family's fissure was real and raw for years following her departure, and her relationship with Robert was strained for many years. The death of the family's first grandchild was a blow that was felt viscerally.

Still, soon after, Michelle delivered Anna into the family. Her birth brought joy and hope to the Jacksons, and they settled into a new normal with Ricky being the only kid left at home. Robert and Kathy could not help but keep Tracy on their minds as she stumbled through the next few years. Still, time heals all wounds, and although this point may have been the most distant the family had been, they would soon begin the journey of coming back closer together. Tracy met and married Jeremiah who had gone to school with Ricky, settled down, and started a family.

Bud finished his enlistment in the Coast Guard in 1997 and moved to North Augusta, South Carolina. It had been a bitter pill to swallow for him. He had taken to military life and had found that he actually enjoyed the lifestyle. He had been able to sail up and down the east coast on his black-hulled buoy tender, completing missions from ice breaking up north to the invasion of Haiti in the Caribbean. He had considered re-enlisting, but he was a new dad. He would have to serve on a 378-foot cutter, which was currently on a European cruise and was docked in Ireland where they were going to fly Bud if he signed the reenlistment papers. He had landed a great duty station at the base on Atlantic Beach at Fort Macon. He decided he would rather ride out his enlistment there and try his hand at a civilian career when his time was up. After his discharge, he was offered an opportunity to work with his father-in-law at his floorcare company in South Carolina. He had tried it out, but the call of the tall pine trees and the morning song of the dove brought him back down that red dirt road to the place he had always called home no matter where he was.

They had been there for less than a year when they decided to move back to North Carolina. Bud yearned to spread his wings and feel like his own man. He had gone straight into the military, and then he had worked for his father-in-law. Bud wanted to be able to feel like he had more control over his family's future. He left Michelle and his daughter Anna in South Carolina and headed north to move back in with his parents while he looked for work and prepared the cabin for his family to live in. He missed them desperately and worked tirelessly to be able to bring them home with him. His days were filled from sun up to sun down with working on the cabin, applying for jobs, or interviewing for jobs. Tracy had moved out, and Ricky was in high school and rarely at home. It was a weird time for Bud because things seemed so different and had changed so much in what to him was such a short amount of time. It seemed like yesterday that he had been a part of this family, and now he had his own to concern himself with primarily.

One morning Bud woke up to an empty house. Ricky had gone off to school, and Robert and Kathy both to work. He came downstairs and made some coffee and ate some breakfast. Bud sat on the couch, watching television, just watching the clock. He had a job interview in a few hours. He did not have time to get started working on anything, then come back home and get cleaned up and dressed, so after breakfast, he took a shower and got ready for his interview. He was nervous, and it seemed that the clock would just not budge. The butterflies in his stomach seemed as though if they decided to all fly in the same direction, they might lift him off of the couch. Still, instead, they fluttered about, causing him to put his hand over his head and lay down on the sofa to try to calm them. He took a deep breath and rubbed his eyes. "I will be glad when this interview is over," he thought.

As he lay there, he heard a motion above him distinctive to anyone that had ever spent any time in the house. There were footsteps right above him. Walking across the floor of Tracy's room, he tracked the steps with his eyes as they walked towards the bedroom door. He leaned up and looked in the driveway. Just his car was there; he was alone. His attention was drawn back into the house by the door to his sister's former room opening and footsteps entering the hall upstairs. Behind the unseen visitor, the door closed. Bud sat up and turned the television off. He closed his eyes and focused on the sounds coming from upstairs. The footsteps crossed the hall, and he heard the door to the room he was sharing with Ricky open. He opened his eyes and looked at the empty stairs. He knew that it was just a few steps down from the doorway until whatever he was hearing would be standing before him. He distinctly heard the shifting of weight from one foot to another there in the doorway, and he heard the hinges to the door creak as the door was being pushed open wider.

The butterflies had subsided, but now Bud sat with his heart in his chest, beating so loud that he was afraid he may miss the sound of the entity's next move. The house grew silent for a moment, and the sound of his heart was all that he could hear. Then, suddenly the crashing boom of the door slamming shook him and the house. The sound reverberated down the stairs and all through the room where Bud sat. It was so loud that he was sure that the door had been torn from its hinges and must be hanging from the frame. Instinctively he leaped to his feet. Thankfully as he had dressed already, he grabbed his keys and fled the house. He locked up the house and ran down the hill to Granny and Pop's house, where he told them what had happened. He felt ridiculous as he told them. Here he was a grown man. He was a veteran out of breath as he sat in his grandparents' living room telling them this fantastic story as though he was a thirteen-year-old that had seen one too many horror movies on Halloween. They thought it was funny themselves and laughed but told him he was, of course, welcomed to stay there with them until it was time for his interview. It would not be the first or last time someone would laugh about one of the family ghost stories, but as Bud sat on their couch, once again feeling the butterflies returning and his heart going back to normal, he did not see the humor in the situation at all.

Chapter 16

Being the youngest can be odd. When you are the youngest child, you have no concept of a world without yourself and your older siblings being in a house together. You are used to sharing everything, waiting in line, usually at the back of the line, in fact. As everyone grows up, though, the youngest finds himself one day as part of a trio, which is precisely what happened to Ricky as he watched Bud and Tracy grow up, move on, and start families. He found himself part of a much smaller family of just himself, Kathy, and Robert. It was odd for them as well. Kathy found herself waking up in the morning with less and less to do as the years progressed. She had fewer lunches to make and fewer stops on the way to work. She found herself sipping coffee in the mornings instead of chasing down wayward socks or yelling for kids to get their teeth brushed.

Ricky had settled into a routine of doing exactly enough to get by at school and working as much as possible. The main thing on his agenda, though, was his girlfriend, Meghan. If he couldn't be with her, then he would tie up the phone line, much to the annoyance of his parents, who had been through the teenage young love stage several times by that point. One night they were talking on the phone, and Ricky was telling Meghan about how at work he had cut his finger. He was cutting watermelons to wrap up for a display in the produce department, and the knife had slipped off the side of the watermelon and cut into his left middle finger. Ricky had wrapped it up pretty well, but it was a deep cut. He was telling her about it, and suddenly Meghan started screaming his name.

"Rick! "Rick!"

"What's wrong?" he asked. Meghan was crying so hard that he couldn't hear her at first.

"Calm down!" Ricky said. "Is everything ok? Are you alright?"

Meghan calmed herself and was silent for a few moments. Then she told him that as he told her about cutting his finger, she heard another voice on the phone. It was a man's voice, and at first, it was very distant. She thought the lines were just crossed, and they were just getting some interference. She didn't want to interrupt what Ricky was saying, so she just listened, but the voice grew a little louder, and she noticed that the man began to comment on what he was saying. The strange voice grew so loud that she started to have trouble hearing Ricky through it. She was about to ask him if he could hear the voice. As he was telling her about the cut to his finger, the voice boomed in her ear, "The blood drained out everywhere!"

Meghan jerked the phone away from her head, almost dropping it, and screamed. Ricky had heard nothing on the phone but the scream. He tried to tell her that it must have just been some mix-up with the lines, but he knew better. If the lines were crossed, he should have heard the voice too. It is doubtful the person on the other end would have gone out of their way to scream such a macabre comment into the phone in response to the lines being crossed. Ricky knew that

Meghan had just met the family secret and had been baptized into the family haunting in a big way.

Chapter 17

Because of Robert's work schedule as a security officer, he often found himself up late, long after Kathy went to sleep. Ricky was the night-time manager at a local grocery store and would work late, most nights getting out between 11:30pm and midnight. He would drive home down the backroads between Raleigh and Durham that still resembled the country that he remembered from his childhood. He would then turn down that dark country road and find the light on in the living room most of the time. Ricky would always smile when he saw this. He was much too geared up to go straight to bed, and he hated coming home to a sleeping house. Ricky's little dog Peanut would greet him at the door with his ears standing straight up and spinning in circles. They would sit up sometimes for many hours into the early morning. Their favorite show was David Letterman. Ricky knew as he was closing the store every night that he could catch the opening monologue if he hurried. They would sit quietly and laugh through it, but when it was over, and the guests came on, they would just sit and talk. Their conversations ranged from history to current events to family matters. It really just depended on the night.

They both treasured the time together, both realizing that good times were not meant to last forever. As it always does, time passes until finally, it caught up to them. Ricky had gotten an apartment in Raleigh, and finally, it was his time to go. Ricky had always had a great relationship with his mom and dad, but it was time for him to spread his wings and fly. He wanted a place to call his own. He worked hard, and he wanted to have a place where he and Meghan could be together alone. They were engaged and could hardly wait until the time when they could be married. Meghan had promised her parents she would wait until she graduated from college, but that seemed like an eternity to the young couple. Ricky was excited to leave but also very nervous about it.

His last night at home, he had to work until eleven o'clock as usual. But, a larger than usual grocery delivery had turned that time into after midnight before he left. When he finally punched out and walked out of the store into the warm summer air, he felt as tired as he ever had. He was off the next day, but he was moving, so he was not looking forward to it, and he knew that rest was going to be in short supply. The combination of excitement and physical labor had really done a number on him, and as he dropped into his car, he felt he could just lay the seat back and sleep right there. He sighed, started his car, and made his usual drive around the store. He needed to ensure that nothing was going on out of the way and all of the doors were closed. He headed home satisfied when he found only raccoons and a cat creeping through the darkness behind the store. He made it home, and as he turned onto the road and crested the hill, he could see the living room lights on through the trees in the distance. "Daddy was still up," he thought.

He was suddenly nervous. He had never really considered how it would be coming in for the last time. He was so exhausted that if he had thought about it, he had forgotten about it until then. He was just not in the mood for an emotional and heartfelt goodbye. Ricky turned off the car and looked at the window where the light was coming from the living room. He knew his dad was sitting on the couch, probably in his underwear with a blanket over his lap and Peanut curled up on the blanket. The nervousness turned to dread as Ricky got out of the car and walked to the house. As he put his key in the lock, he heard Peanut hit the floor and, in his mind, could see the little sentry standing with his radar up as Daddy would say. He opened the door, and the scene was just as he had imagined.

"Come on in and sit down," Daddy said. "Must have been a big truck tonight."

"I'm so tired," Ricky said. "I think I am going to just go straight to bed," he said as he came in and shut the door behind him. "I am beat."

He could see the disappointed look spread across his dad's face. It had been just like he had thought on the ride home. He had wanted to have one more night with his boy before he was gone. Robert had wanted just one more Letterman Show, one more corny joke, and one more conversation about whatever his son wanted to talk about. He had been through this before, and he knew that although they could still talk and see each other, it would never be just the same as it had been. He faked a smile.

"I get it, man, been there, cowboy," he said. "Go grab some sleep."

Ricky walked past him, and Robert stuck out his hand as he always did when Ricky went to bed. Ricky took his hand in his and squeezed. "Night, pop," he said, and he walked across the room and up the stairs. Ricky could hear Peanut's little paws tapping the floor right behind him as he climbed the stairs and went into his room. He closed the door behind him, pulled off his tie and his shirt. Being so tired, Ricky didn't even turn the television on. He sat on the side of his bed and kicked his shoes and socks off. As he stood up to slip his pants off, he heard the distinct sound of footsteps coming up the back stairs. Ricky stopped and stood back up. He pulled his pants back up in anticipation of his company. He was sure it was his dad coming to have a heart-to-heart about him leaving home. He again felt the dread of an emotional meeting between him and his dad. He was at the age where he was at the zenith of being uncomfortable with any emotion other than that which was approved by the WWE.

The footsteps reached the landing at the top of the stairs and stopped right in front of his door. "Here we go," Ricky thought. Hugs and kisses here in the middle of the night with his dad. How embarrassing? But after a few seconds, he heard the footsteps going back down the stairs. "Daddy must have lost his nerve and gone to bed," he thought. He slipped his pants off, turned the light off, which was by the door, and he walked over to his bed once more. Ricky had not even gotten in bed yet when he again heard the steps coming up the stairs.

"Oh man, this is going to be awkward," he thought, and he sat down on his bed in the dark and heard the steps come again to the landing right outside of his door. He was determined not to answer the door unless he knocked. Ricky felt the best strategy was to try to wait this out and just move on. Surely, he would see the light out now under the door and know he was in bed now. It seemed to work because it was just a few seconds later when again, he heard his dad walk back down the stairs. Although he had now twice dodged having to face his emotions, he felt so bad. This was obviously hard for him, and it was now apparent to Ricky that he was not making it easier for his dad. He lay down in bed and got under the covers feeling like a pretty big jerk for not hanging out with him when he got home. "What would an hour have hurt?" he thought. He lay there for a minute or two and had just about decided to get up and go back downstairs when he once more heard the footsteps again falling on those old oak stairs leading up to his bedroom door.

Ricky had taken all he could stand, and as he listened to the steps drawing closer, he could see his dad - an emotional wreck. His mind drifted back to the night that he had walked through the woods to say goodbye to Bud. Ricky remembered his dad's gnarled face as Robert tried to speak but only sobbed. He didn't like how it made him feel to see his dad like that, but the thought that he was putting him through that was too much for him to bear. Ricky threw the covers off of himself and threw his legs over the side of the bed. The footsteps reached the door as he stood to go and open it. Ricky had decided to just go ahead and embrace the awkward moment that he had been avoiding and give the old man some time with his baby boy.

As he stood up, though, before he could even get into a straightened position, Ricky froze. In the silence of his room, he could hear the footsteps continue. They were not going down the stairs this time, but they were coming across the room towards him. His heart leaped into his throat as he stared into the darkness of his room, illuminated only by the moonlight coming through the mini blinds. Through the shadows, he could see the closed bedroom door and the shadow of the pile of dirty clothes in the corner. He could see that he was alone, yet his ears were telling him that he was not. He quickly dropped back down into the bed and covered his head with his blanket. He thought of crying out but stopped himself. "Last night," he began telling himself. "Last night." He heard the footsteps come across the room right up to the side of his bed and stop. The room again filled with silence broken only by the low growl of Peanut, who was curled up at the end of the bed.

It took him a few minutes until he got up the nerve to peek out and see that just like before, there was nothing there. There were no more sounds, just the night. He crept out from his sanctuary of his blanky and his five-pound rat terrier and ran across the room to the light switch and turned it on. He slowly cracked his door and looked down the stairs. The only light he could see was from the night light at the bottom of the stairs that had been there since they lived in the house to keep the kids from killing themselves on the stairs during a late-night bathroom trip. He closed the door back and retreated to the safety of his bed. Ricky spent his last night in the house under the covers with the light on like he was eight years old again.

The next morning when he got up, Kathy was in the kitchen cooking breakfast. It was his last morning at home, and she wanted to say goodbye in her way too. Robert was sleeping in his room as Ricky passed the door. It was cracked, and the sound of what could be mistaken for a small yet vicious grizzly bear was coming out. He was surprised that his mom was able to sleep at all. He took a seat at the kitchen table, and after a little small talk with his mom, he asked her how daddy was.

"He's fine," she said.

"Oh, I thought I heard him come upstairs last night; I thought he wanted to talk," Ricky said.

"No, I heard you come in last night. He came right to bed after you went upstairs," she said.

He didn't ask her if she had heard anything else. Honestly, he still felt guilty. Not only had he not slept very well the night before, but what his mom told him was confirmation that his dad had stayed up just to see him.

Ricky was the baby of the family, and when he left home, it was the end of a chapter in Robert and Kathy's life. Their time of raising kids had ended, and a new chapter was beginning for them. Their time as empty nesters were dawning, and they faced it with their own anxieties and worries. Robert had always told the kids that they were on the 18/15 program, meaning they had 18 years and 15 minutes until they had to move out of the house. But, becoming empty nesters was more difficult than they would let on. The truth was that Robert and Kathy loved their kids dearly and hated to see each one of them leave. Still, they also wanted them to be productive members of society who could make it independently. They knew all too well that the world could be harsh, and they would not always be there to help them out.

The Jackson family. Back row second from left is Willie, holding Robert. Beside him is his wife, Lee, and his sister, Rosa. Clifton is to the far right.

Willie and Lee on their wedding day

Baby Elizabeth Jackson at burial. Lee would swear all of her life that she heard the angels come for her.

It seemed like destiny for Robert and Kathy to be together from a young age.

Kathy Tripp

Robert Jackson

Robert and Kathy in front of the cotton mill

Robert and Kathy young and in love

Robert and Kathy's wedding day

Both took their vows serious and began their marriage with prayerful hope

Robert and Kathy graduated as man and wife

Robert and Kathy waiting for Bud to arrive

Robert stepping over Bud as he works on the cabin

The Jackson kids taking a break as the cabin is being built

The remodel of the old farmhouse was a challenging time for Robert and Kathy

The Jackson Family on vacation

Chapter 18

"One by one, their seats were emptied.
One by one, they went away.
Now the family is parted.
Will it be complete one day?
Will the circle be unbroken
By and by, by and by?
Is a better home awaiting
In the sky, in the sky?"

"Will the Circle Be Unbroken" by Ada R. Habershon

After Ricky left home, Robert and Kathy found themselves once more just as they had started, a duo. It was something that they had to adjust to. The past few years for them had been a practice run because Ricky had really not been one to hang around the house. He had been at his friend's house, or Meghan's house, or at work. They had always figured that things would feel about like they had when he was still living at home, but they were wrong. There was an immediate change in the feeling of the house. It seemed a little darker and a little colder, not because of the ghost but because of the kids' absence. The clothes Kathy had complained for years about having to pick up and wash disappeared, and Robert didn't have to worry about someone leaving a door unlocked.

It was a strange time of adjustment for them. Although Robert and Kathy had been married several years before Bud was born, they seemed unused to being just a couple. They spent a lot of time talking about the changes in their lives, and they made some decisions. First, they decided that they had worked very hard and were going to retire a soon as they were able to. Second, they agreed that they had gone without for so long that they would start to do the things they wanted to do. Because they had been so poor when raising small kids, they had learned to live a very frugal life. They were now looking at being able to save money instead of living paycheck to paycheck. The small farmhouse they had raised their kids in was almost paid for, and they were both making more money than they ever had.

They decided that what they really wanted to do was travel. Robert and Kathy thought, "Why wait until our health prevents us from seeing the world?" They both had plenty of vacation time, so off they went. The kids had a hard time keeping up with them during those years. They traveled to Europe, Alaska, Hawaii, and all of the lower forty-eight states. They drove, they took cruises, and they crisscrossed the country by air. They saw things that they could have only imagined. The young man and woman who walked across Durham High School's graduation stage as newlyweds could have never imagined that they would look out over the Pacific Ocean from Diamond Head or see the Tower of London. They made a lifetime worth of memories with each other and added those to the memories of raising the kids. They marched on towards their golden years with a new sense of purpose. They were going to make every moment last together until the very end.

It was just the two of them, so traveling was easy except for finding someone to watch their two small dogs, Minnie and Sophie. Bud lived in Raleigh, but he had begun a career as a Deputy Sheriff in Durham, so he parked his patrol car at the house. He would drive to their home every morning to switch cars and then again at the end of his shift. It was easy for him to let the dogs out to the bathroom and feed them while they were gone. Bud did not mind doing this for them since he was there anyway. He now had a second daughter Lauren, and of the three of Kathy and Robert's children, he felt the most connected to the old farmhouse and the land surrounding it. This is where he had spent his formative years. The white farmhouse had provided his wife Michelle a place to stay when her family moved away, and she decided to stay with him. It was the little cabin his parents had built that served as his first home with his wife and had been the place he came home to when he moved his young family back from South Carolina.

One morning Kathy was waiting for Bud when he pulled into the driveway to get his patrol car. She came out on the front porch with a sausage biscuit wrapped in aluminum foil in her hand.

"Morning," she said as he walked towards her.

"Morning," Bud replied, "Thanks for breakfast." It was a regular thing for his mom to make him breakfast, and a homemade sausage biscuit sounded great right about then. He had to wake up so early to get suited up and then drive a county over to work, so he had little time to fix himself anything in the mornings. The only problem with mom's cooking was that when she cooked something, she really cooked it. Often when she would make him a biscuit in the mornings, he would unfold the aluminum foil as he pulled out of the driveway and set it on the console by the air conditioning. The steam would pour off of the biscuit as the cool air hit it. It would not be safe to eat until he got all the way downtown, and he would eat it in the parking lot before going in for morning line-up. She liked her food hot, and more than once, one of the kids, if not careful, would take a huge bite of dinner and lose half of the skin inside of their mouths to third-degree burns. It took nothing away from the flavor, though, and a home-cooked meal from Kathy Jackson was much sought after among the kids.

"Me and your daddy are thinking about riding off this weekend. Do you think you could come by and check on the dogs for us?" She hated to bother him on the weekend when she knew it was easier for him to watch after them during the week. Still, she and Robert had gotten the urge to go "scooter pootin," as they called it.

"Sure," Bud said. "Would it be alright if we just stayed over here for the weekend?" he asked. Bud loved to be in the country, and he wanted his girls to experience the life he had lived. He also wanted them to spend some time in the house, so he figured it would be a good opportunity to do both.

"I hate for y'all to have to do that," she said.

"No, it's no problem. In fact, I have been wanting to get the girls out here more, and it would be cool to let them sleep in the house so they could really see how we grew up."

It was settled, and when Friday evening came around, as Bud pulled his patrol car down the long dirt road, he could see that his parents' car was already gone, and Michelle's car was in the driveway. He smiled as he pulled up to the house where his wife sat on the front porch watching his two little girls run around in the yard, squealing and laughing as little girls will do. They ran to him as he got out of his car, and he carried them, one in each arm, to the porch. Bud sat them down, and off they ran back to their game. Darkness descended through the trees, and he sat down with his wife to watch the kids play as long as they could until it was time to go inside.

As the shadow of nighttime fell longer on the little white house and the crickets chirped in time with the croaking of the frogs, Bud thought about the many days he played outside until the very last minute. Bud was glad his mom had asked him to watch the dogs, and he was glad he could spend the night with the sounds of the country instead of the sounds of the city humming around him.

Chapter 19

After dinner and baths, Bud and Michelle watched television with the girls for a while and then took them up to his old room and put them to bed. They left their door open slightly and made sure that the night light at the bottom of the stairs was on. They got ready for bed themselves and went into the master bedroom to settle down for the night. There was no TV in the room, and they were not quite ready to go to sleep, so they left the light on and read for a while. The bedroom door was propped open with an 18-inch tall concrete statue of a Confederate soldier that Robert had painted. The door stayed open even when it was just Robert and Kathy at home. They had always left the door open to hear the kids if they needed them, and old habits die hard. The door being open was fine with Bud because he wanted to make sure he could hear the girls, too, if they needed him, and he remembered how good his dad had insulated the house.

"Do you think the girls will be alright?" Michelle asked.

"Oh my God, here we go."

"What?" she said

"You are always worried about nothing. I grew up in this house, and I survived."

"Those stairs are so steep, though. I worry about them trying to come down in the middle of the night and falling."

"They will be fine," Bud said.

Michelle lay back in the bed and put the book across her chest. She looked at the ceiling and then began to giggle.

"What?" Bud asked, looking at her quizzically.

"Nothing," she said, looking over at him. "It's just you are the one that is always so protective of them, and now we have totally flipped roles. Usually, I'm the one saying they will be fine."

They went back to reading but eventually, they both had put down their books and were just talking. Soon the conversation turned to the "ghosts" of the house.

"Do you think the ghost will get them?" Michelle asked as she tickled Bud's side and made the wooooooooooo ghost noise. Bud jerked away from her and rolled over away from her.

"What's wrong?" she asked. "Scared I am going to make the ghost mad?"

"I don't know about the ghost, but you are pissing me off," Bud said.

"Really?" Michelle said, "Are you getting mad? I'm just messing with you".

Bud chaffed at her ribbing him about the ghost because it was something he could not prove her wrong about. Also, he bristled at the insinuation that he and his family had either imagined everything or were just telling lies.

"We aren't all just lying about it," Bud said.

"I don't know why you are getting so mad? I am just messing around with you about it," Michelle said. "I just think you guys all were looking for some reason to think the house was haunted, and when anything happened that was strange, you guys hung it on a ..." Before she could finish her thought, the door to the bedroom slammed shut with a booming thud. Bud leaped from the bed and moved quickly to the door. He flung it open, expecting to find a physical person there, but there was nothing. The hall was empty, and the house was dark. He was sure that there had to be something there that had slammed the door. He looked down at his feet and saw the heavy statue that had been propping the door open on its side several inches from where it had stood. It was as if someone kicked it out of the way to allow the door to be slammed. The silent house calmed his initial anxiety. He had expected a fight, but there was no way anyone had been there.

As he realized what had happened, he looked over at Michelle, who was sitting up in bed. A look of bewilderment and fear hung on her face as she looked back at him. Bud walked around the house to make sure everything was alright and came back to the door. He opened the door back up, and he sat the statue back up against it. He tested it several times by trying to close the door with the statue in place, but it was tough to do as the statue slid across the floor in front of the door like an anchor. To make the statue fall, the door would have to be really slammed with a lot of force unless the statue was moved first.

"I tried to tell you," he said to Michelle as he got into bed. "I told you. Sometimes stuff happens here that you just can't explain." No longer in the mood to play around or rib him about it, Michelle agreed.

"I think we have had enough excitement for the night," she said, "Let's go to bed."

Bud laughed. "Yeah, I think so."

"Maybe you need to go and check on the girls one more time," Michelle said as Bud settled in bed beside her.

"They are fine," Bud said. "Nothing here is going to hurt them."

"I'm just so worried that they are going to fall down those stairs, though," she said.

"You worry too much," Bud said as he leaned over and turned off the light.

Darkness had barely covered the room when they heard a booming crash from the stairs. The distinct sound of banging, thumping, and flailing sounds came front the staircase, and in their hearts, they knew it was the sound of one of the girls falling down. As soon as the sound had begun, Bud had flung himself out of bed and towards the door. Still, he trailed Michelle, who was already making a beeline through the house towards the stairs. He could see her silhouette in the faint light of the nightlight at the bottom of the stairs and almost crashed into her as she came to an abrupt stop. Bud reached her and stopped by her side. At the bottom of the stairs, where they had expected to find one of their young daughters hurt and scared, they found there was absolutely nothing there.

The silence of the house was palpable and seemed to pulsate around. They stood in awe of what they had just experienced together. No words were necessary, but the silence was suddenly broken by a low growl coming from their feet. They looked down in unison to see the small terrier Sophie staring with them at the bottom of the stairs. The hair on her back stood straight up, her head was down, and her teeth were visible as she growled at something that they could not see. Without a word, Bud and Michelle ascended the stairs and found the girls sleeping soundly. They each picked up one of the girls and brought them downstairs, where they laid them on the bed, and Michelle made a pallet on the floor. They moved the girls to the pallet and huddled together.

As they once again tried to settle down for the night, Bud stared up at the ceiling. He came to two realizations. First, Michelle would never doubt him or anyone else in his family again when they talked about an experience with the ghost in the house. The second was that whatever was here in the house was surely watching them from some dark corner and probably laughing at them as they spent the night on the floor huddled in fear.

Chapter 20

Robert and Kathy continued to travel constantly. They had both now worked for the state for many years and had accrued large amounts of vacation time. With the kids gone and the little house paid for, they also found that they had money to spend, which was a new experience for two people that had known the disease of poverty since childhood. They often reflected on how blessed they were and how they could have never imagined all of those years that they struggled how good life could one day be for them. They wished they would have had the extra money when the kids were small, but it was just not how life had worked out. But they often stood together looking out over some wonder and wished the kids could see what they were seeing. The Grand Canyon, Diamond Head, the majestic views in Alaska; they saw them all but wished they could have been able to share these sights with their kids.

During these years of travel, Bud kept a watch out for their two little dogs. They lost Sophie, the small terrier, to cancer during this time, leaving just their Dachshund named Minnie. She was a boisterous little dog, and generally, she charged any visitors to the house barking and nipping at their heels at times. The nails on her paws clicking against the hard floors as she came. She was an older dog when Robert and Kathy had adopted her. Although she was not a family favorite, they loved her dearly. Robert would hold her and say that nobody else would have wanted her, so he was glad that he got her.

One night when they were off on another adventure, Bud once again finished his shift and headed out to change cars before going home. He had been held up at work and was late getting off. He was generally able to avoid that happening in his duties, but occasionally it could not be helped. When he had walked out of the courthouse where his office was, he looked up at menacing skies that seemed to be holding back a vicious storm. It looked like it would break at any moment. Lightening was streaking the night sky, and the sound of thunderclaps grew closer and closer. A light rain began falling as he got into his car and as he drove to his parents' house, but the storm had still not opened up. As he drove down the road to the house and turned the corner to the driveway, lightning illuminated the house's silhouette. He needed to run inside to grab something before he headed home, and as he put his car in park, the bottom opened up, and the rain began to fall heavily. Cursing, he ran across the yard to the porch to get out of the rain, and he tried to shake some of it off as he put the key in the door and entered the dark house.

When he stepped inside, everything was deathly quiet, with the only interruption of that silence being the thunder. The thunder clapped again as he stood in the door, and again silence fell upon the house. He reached for what he needed in a hurry to head home when he heard the pattering of paws and the clicking of nails running from the kitchen into the living room where he was standing. He stood there for a moment and waited for Minnie to appear at his feet. She was a solid black dog and close to the ground, so in the dark, she could be right up on you before you could see her. The sound was so distinctive that he began to stoop to touch her when she got to his feet.

He pulled his hand back though and stood upright as it suddenly occurred to him that Minnie had recently died. They no longer had a dog at all! He grabbed what he needed and retreated back out of the door. He ran back out to his car, not even wanting to look back at the house, afraid of what he may see. Drenched, he fumbled for his keys and started the car. As he backed out of the driveway, the lightning flashed again, illuminating the house just as it did when he had driven up to it moments before. A chill ran down his spine as he pulled out of the driveway and drove away. After years of experiencing strange things in the house, it should have been expected when paranormal things happened. Still, things never happened when they were expected. Things always seemed to happen the moment that someone had their guard down.

Several years later, Bud came to this realization when he stopped at the house for lunch to grab a bite to eat. Robert and Kathy had gone to the beach, which was their favorite place to disappear for a few days. Bud followed his usual routine. He came into the house, went straight to the kitchen, and opened the refrigerator to see what kind of leftovers his mom had kept for him. Then he would move on to the cabinets scrounging for something to eat. His mom always kept something around for him to eat at lunch since he came frequently. He always felt like a teenager who was just getting home from school when mom was not there, and he was searching for food.

He had settled on lunch, heated it up, and sat at the table watching a video on his phone when he heard a noise. He had almost finished eating when he heard it, and he set the phone down and listened intently to what it was. It sounded like it had come from upstairs. All of the experiences from all of the years he had lived there began to come back to him. The hair on his arms and the back of his neck stood on end, and he became very tense. He was not going to be surprised by something this time, he decided.

Years of being a law enforcement officer and combat engineer had conditioned him to respond when confronted with a threat, and he felt himself enter into that zone. Suddenly, the defrost fan on the refrigerator kicked on and startled him. It broke the tension, and he looked at the refrigerator and then out of the window where he could see that the wind was blowing. Bud could literally feel his muscles relaxing, and he laughed at himself for being on edge. He figured he had just heard the wind, so he turned his video back on and continued watching it while finishing his lunch.

A moment later, just as he became relaxed again, he heard a louder noise. This time it was definitely coming from upstairs. It was as if something heavy had been dropped or some heavy blow had been placed against one of the walls upstairs. The sound was so distinct that he thought for a moment that maybe his parents had not gone to the beach after all. Maybe Mom had gone off, and Dad was upstairs doing something when he came in and had not heard him.

That would explain why the car was gone, and everything was locked up.

"Hey, Daddy," he called out.

He didn't want him to come down the stairs and be startled by him if he didn't know he was there. He waited but received no response to his call. Bud got up and walked into the living room. There was no one there. He walked to the bottom of the stairs and looked up. No one.

"Daddy," he called again. Again, receiving no response, so he went back to the kitchen to finish up his lunch. Bud turned his phone back on and settled back into his video.

Now he was thinking it was the ghost, but he also knew that he would not let some bump upstairs keep him from his few moments of relaxation he had for the day. No sooner than he had settled down though he heard the noise again. He turned his phone off and listened. He was curious now more than afraid as he listened for another noise. That curiosity was quickly replaced with fear as the next noise he heard was clearly the sound of someone walking down the stairs. The hollow thud, thud, thud of footfalls on the narrow stairs was distinctive to anyone who had lived there and heard it a million times over the years. The steps came to the bottom of the stairs, and he could hear them now coming through the living room. The sound of Daddy's recliner being moved as if something had bumped into it was clear as he sat listening in the kitchen. The steps came to the door of the living room where he should have been looking at the source of the noise but was instead staring at emptiness.

Bud had had enough and stood up, put his phone in his pocket, and threw the rest of his lunch in the garbage.

"Ok," he said aloud, "I'm leaving."

He made his way through the living room, being careful to look straight ahead. He avoided looking around too much as the image of the gray man that his dad had described so many years ago was running through his mind. It was an image that had frightened him for years, and he didn't want to take the chance of seeing something like that. Bumps and sounds were one thing, but he knew that he did not want to add to those experiences with an image impossible to erase from his memory. Whatever was there was enjoying its privacy while his parents were away, and he was satisfied to let it have the house for now. He decided that maybe he should bring his lunch from home for the next few days, at least until he heard from his parents that they were home and he wouldn't have to be alone in the house.

Chapter 21

In the years after the kids moved out, Robert and Kathy settled into a pretty steady routine of working and traveling. Kathy became an unquestionable expert at her job. She constantly had to fend off calls for her to move into different roles taking on more responsibility. Robert had long since been a fixture at the school. He had also turned down the opportunity for advancement even though it would have meant that he could have stopped working the crazy night and day shifts he had always had to work. They were very content with their lives and were eyeing their next phase of retirement.

When Robert worked nights, he would often be home by himself during the day while Kathy was at work. He began to work on the property, raking leaves and clearing land. He also began working on a project Jeep that he had purchased and even had a garage built in the backyard. He tried his best to stay busy and stay off the couch, but he was always lonely there by himself during the day. When he worked days, they rode to work together and had lunch together. Kathy would go to her mom's house, Granny Tripp, near the School of Science and Math to make sure she was set up and had what she needed. Even after she passed away, Kathy would still wait for Robert to get off so they could ride together to work and home.

When Robert worked nights, though, Kathy found herself alone in the house down the long path in the country. There were times when she would be just fine with this. When she had her little dogs, she felt safer, but she found herself alone again after the last one died. Her only neighbors were far enough down the road that you could not see their house until the dead of winter when the trees had lost all their leaves, and Robert's parents no longer lived in their house at the bottom of the hill. His dad had passed away several years before, and his mom was living in a skilled nursing facility in Durham. She felt alone and nervous many times but never let on to Robert that it bothered her.

On more than one occasion, she would be awakened in the middle of the night by the sound of footsteps crossing the floor above her in the room where her two sons grew up but now was full of boxes and memories. She would lay awake, looking up at the popcorn-blown ceiling and listening to the sound of pacing feet above her. She liked to sleep with the covers barely on her and at least one leg totally uncovered but, on these nights, she retreated in the sheets and blanket like a turtle and struggled to sleep until she could either see the sun peeking through the blinds or she heard the crackling of rocks on the road signaling that Robert was home.

It was not until they had long been retired when one night Robert awakened her and quietly whispered, "Listen." They lay together and listened to the pacing of feet in the room above them.

"I have been listening to it for a while now," Robert softly said, as if not to give their presence away to the intruder. It was there in the darkness that Kathy told him of the many nights that she had heard the footsteps above her. Robert felt a tinge of guilt for not being there when she was scared. After all, he was supposed to be her protector. But, protect her from what, he thought. He knew he was ridiculous to feel this way, but even after all of the years they had been together, Robert still felt like a teenaged boy who had found out that someone had been mean or rude to his girl. It was the first time he had ever felt anger towards the spirit or spirits in the house.

"I'm sorry I wasn't here," he said, breaking the tension in the room as the silent house betrayed only the sound of the walking.

"You had to work, baby," Kathy said. "I was fine." Robert wasn't so sure, but what could he do now other than always be with her, which is exactly what he planned to do anyway. What he did not know was that the footsteps had been scary at times, but after a while, they had just become more of an annoyance to Kathy. She had another experience, though, that she did not want to tell him about.

Chapter 22

One summer night, when Robert was working, Kathy had been working hard herself. She had been working in the yard in the evening since the days were long and was exhausted. She had more work to do, though, as she stood on the front porch looking out at the flower bed and the well-trimmed grass feeling a sense of accomplishment. She had laundry to do still, and she was not looking forward to it. Their washer was broken, and she had been using the washing machine in Granny Jackson's house at the bottom of the hill. Granny had recently had a health scare and had been sent to a skilled nursing facility to rehab. She had high hopes that she would be able to come home soon, so they had tried to keep her house ready for her. Unfortunately, she would not make it back home from this trip to the nursing home and would spend her last few years there.

Kathy looked up at the rolling black storm clouds visible in the last bit of daylight and sighed. "No rest for the weary," she thought. She quickly grabbed her clothes basket and walked briskly down the hill and through the backdoor to the washer and dryer. She loaded the washing machine with clothes and soap and adjusted the knobs. As she turned to go, a crashing boom of thunder shook the house, and she knew she better hurry. As she crested the hill, the heavens opened and soaked her before she could reach the porch. Tired, wet, and dreading the trip back to granny's house in the storm to put the clothes in the dryer, she took a few moments to get something to eat and relax as the storm raged around the house. The time to switch the clothes to the dryer neared, so she decided she would get a shower so she could relax when she got back and get ready for bed.

Kathy went into the bathroom and began her shower. Even in the bathroom, away from any large windows, the thunder still boomed so loud that she could almost feel its vibrations on her skin. As she enjoyed the warm water, she thought she better not take too long in case the lights were to go out. She had not grabbed a flashlight or set up any candles anywhere, so if the power kicked off now, she would find herself grouping through the house naked, trying to find some source of light. "Shoot," she thought. The shower was so nice after a hard day, and she hated to give it up. Rarely did she neglect to prepare for almost any scenario, and she was mad at herself for not setting everything up already. She reluctantly turned the water off and put her hand on the shower curtain to pull it back when her body became tense and fear crept over her. She felt something; a presence in the shower with her. She felt watched and vulnerable suddenly and was momentarily scared to pull the curtain back.

She steeled herself to the task, and after a moment of hesitation, she threw the curtain back to an empty room. Momentary relief was shattered by the sudden stench of dirt, tobacco, and body odor! It was the same smell she had smelled so many years before when she and Robert had fallen asleep on the floor. She felt fear, but also, she felt violated. It was as if the spirit of an old farmer took the opportunity to be a voyeur while she showered. She quickly dressed and ran out of the room. The living room was devoid of the scent, and again, her relief was shattered when the smell enveloped her there also. She decided that it was time to flee the house and switch her clothes to the dryer. There was no way she was walking, so she grabbed her car keys and ran out of the front door, through the downpour, and into her car.

In the car soaking wet, she rested her head on the steering wheel and stopped herself from crying. She had only really felt this kind of fear the first time she smelled the farmer, mostly because she could tell someone was there but could not see him. It was like there was an invisible man in the room with them, and it unnerved her. This time though, it seemed like the spirit was purposely invading her privacy, and there were so many questions bouncing around in her head as she looked up from the steering wheel to the front porch. Through the rain, she could see the porch illuminated by the porch light and the light from the living room. She sighed, feeling safe again but wondering how she would get up the nerve to go back into the house and go to sleep as if nothing happened.

She put the car in reverse and backed out to the road. She put the car in drive, and as she drove by the house and down the road, she was once again notified of the presence she had been confronted with inside as her nostrils were filled with the same rancid odor. The darkness of the road behind the car was lit up, and the sheets of rain were illuminated red as she slammed down on the brakes. She grabbed the door handle and opened the door to make her escape but stopped. Kathy was no wallflower, and she always blushed when Robert talked about how tough she was and how she was of "pioneer stock," but she knew it was true. Her fear turned to anger, and she took her foot off the brake and proceeded down the road towards her mother-in-law's house. "I guess you're coming too, huh," she asked the empty car.

When she ran into the house to change the clothes over to the dryer, she expected her stalker to go with her, but he did not. When she went back to the car, the only scent was of the Glade air freshener hanging from the air vent. She drove back up the road to her house, and purposefully did not hesitate to jump out of the car and bound up the steps and into the house. She strode through the living room confidently as if to show the spirit that it was her house and he was the one that was out of place, not her. The power never went out but did flicker once or twice. She watched a little television and went to bed. She had tried to have as normal of an evening as she could, but she felt watched the entire night. Sleep was in short supply until she heard Robert's Jeep sloshing through the mud puddles in the driveway the next morning.

Chapter 23

"And there was war in heaven: Michael and his angels fought against the dragon; and the dragon fought and his angels,

And prevailed not; neither was their place found any more in heaven.

And the great dragon was cast out, that old serpent, called the Devil, and Satan, which deceiveth the whole world: he was cast out into the earth, and his angels were cast out with him."

Revelations 12:7-9

He sat bolt upright in the middle of the night, sweat dripping from his nose in the pitch black and heaving. His chest felt tight, and the adrenaline still ran through him like high-octane jet fuel. Meghan sat up beside him and put her hand on his back.

"Are you ok, Rick?" she asked.

"Yeah," he said through deep breaths.

"The same dream again?"

He shook his head up and down in the darkness and grunted in the affirmative.

"I'll be ok, baby," he said. "Just go back to bed. You know the drill. I will be alright."

She sat up, hugged him, and kissed him lightly on the cheek.

"I love you," she said. "You are here, and everything is fine."

He reached up and touched her hand and kissed it.

"I know, go back to bed."

He threw his feet over the side of the bed and saw her snuggling back down into bed as he opened the door and headed downstairs. He turned the light on above the stove. It was too early for a big light, and he looked at the clock on the microwave; 3:07am. He rubbed his eyes and thought about what a long day it was going to be. No need to fight it though, sleep was not a possibility for the rest of this night, and he knew it. Almost ninja-like, he filled the coffee maker with Folgers and water and stood watching the black gold pour into the coffee pot. He knew he wouldn't be getting any more sleep, but Meghan was sure to already be asleep again by now.

When the coffee was made, he took the steaming cup out on the back patio and sat listening to the night critters call to each other. The occasional car drove down the road through the trees. The whole world was sleeping, it seemed, but he was so wired he felt restless just sitting there. The minutes and hours ticked by there in the darkness as he replayed the dream over and over in his mind. It was the same one as always. He had had it for years now, and it was always the same, over and over. He called it a dream, but it was truly a nightmare.

Above him, he faintly heard the alarm go off and knew it was now 6am. Meghan stirred, and he wished that he had been mindful of the time and turned the alarm off for her. It was always better to be woken up gently by someone than have some annoying alarm blaring in your ear. Her footsteps crossed the bedroom, and he lost the sound of her through the floor and walls, but he knew where she was. Moments later, the sliding glass door behind him opened, and she peeked out at him, eyes tired and hair a mess.

"I thought I would find you here," Meghan said.

"I couldn't sleep, and I didn't want to bother you," replied Rick.

"What time did you wake up?" she asked.

"About three," Rick answered.

She came out on the patio with him and sat in the chair beside him. She took his hand in hers, and they sat in silence for a few minutes.

"Do you want to talk about it?"

He thought for a moment and looked over at her. Talk about it, he thought. What is there to talk about? It was literally the same exact dream he had been having for years.

"I'm ok, baby," he said as he reached over and put his other hand on top of hers. "It is the same dream I have always had."

"I wonder what it means? If it means anything? Do you think it is a memory?" Meghan questioned.

In his mind, the replay began. It flashed through his mind like a home movie. The scene is "the cabin," as his family called it - the two-room house his dad and mom built out in the country when he was just a little boy. His memories were good in the cabin. Poverty had made them endure things that most would think were awful times, but you don't know that there is a difference when you are poor and a child. He could see

Christmas trees in the corner, and he could see mama cooking by the stove. He could remember mornings sitting by a small kitchen table when it was so cold he and his brother and sister sat wrapped in blankets as their breath streamed out in front of them like smoke.

The cabin had always brought good feelings and memories until the dream began years ago. It starts in the living room. The cabin is dark, and the only light that can be seen is the illumination from the bathroom light that mama would leave on and crack the door. This served as her nightlight for many years. The perspective of the illuminated doorway is viewed from the far side of the room where mama and daddy would have slept. The dream also begins with a strange feeling of dread. Something is coming. He can't tell who is there with him or if he is alone. He can't move, though, and all he can do is look at the doorway as the tension builds. Then in the doorway in the faint light, a mist begins to form. Black as smoke, the mist swirls and grows. He can feel the fear build in him like a symphony moving towards the crescendo. He can't move, though. He can't look away; he just can look. It forms and becomes a black figure in the doorway, and the fear is unbearable. As it becomes intolerable, the figure moves towards him, and that is when he wakes up.

"Nothing like that ever happened to me there. Plus, I was really young when we lived there."

She half-smiles and stands and gives him a kiss.

"I am going to get my shower, Hun. I'm sorry that happens to you. Maybe one day they will stop. It has been a long time since the last time, hasn't it?"

"I'd say over six months. Maybe a year." The dreams were like that. He knew that he may have the same dream, or nightmare, tomorrow night and the next. Or, it could be in a month or a year before the next one, but they were always the same. Always the door and always the figure. He was always trapped there looking at the black form coming towards him, and he always woke up at the same time. It was vivid.

"Ok, baby, I am right behind you."

Meghan disappeared into the house once more and left him alone on the patio. By now, the birds were singing, and he could see a robin flitting around the beechnut tree in the backyard. Rick stood up and sighed as he contemplated the day. Maybe he should go talk to someone about it, he thought. But what would he say? Occasionally he had this weird, scary dream. The notion seemed kind of weak to him and rubbed him the wrong way. He hadn't told any other soul in the world about the dream other than Meghan. Honestly, he doubts he would have ever told her had she not been awakened so often over the years by it herself. Having to comfort him in the dead of night had won her the inside scoop on his terror, he supposed. Rick took one last deep breath, looked around at the birds, and put it back where it belonged - in the back of his mind until it happened again, and he went inside to get a shower and shave. Determined to have a great day, he would suffer through this nightmare for several more years until he learned its origin.

Chapter 24

Bud and Ricky trudged down the hill on an overgrown path that used to be worn down to a wide clear path. Little feet raced back and forth down this path for many years, up and down the hill over and over to fetch water, to see Granny and Pop, or to visit Bud and Michelle. Time marches on, and none of those things were down the hill any longer. Now the path was barely trodden and was most often used to cut across the bottom of the property. They could head north to the power lines and onto the lake or head to the Rogers Plantation. The plantation was now just rock foundations and sunken graves but once was, in their lifetime, a scattering of abandoned buildings in the middle of the woods. They passed the rotting cabin on their left as they headed into the tree line.

It was hard not to see history in motion as they walked by the small cabin they once called home. They passed the little cabin in silence. Ricky didn't like to walk by it any longer. He had fond memories of the cabin. This is where he and mama spent so much time together when he was small, and he could still see her standing there on the side porch announcing that dinner was done. It was not bad memories but a bad dream that made him wary of the cabin.

They walked on past and down towards the pond, picked up the power lines, and crossed the creek. After crossing the creek, they turned back north. They headed to the lake, where they skirted the water until the foliage opened up, and they could see the path leading to the old plantation grounds. They passed unmarked graves on their left where slaves were buried. These graves had been moved once before but never marked by the state. They wondered if, in the bureaucratic takeover of the old Neuse River basin to create Falls Lake, anyone had even noted these poor souls' new resting ground. The terrain began to lift upward. Soon, they came to another clearing where they passed the cinderblock skeleton of an old tobacco barn.

Then they arrived at the foundation and piles of rotting wood that was once a two-story home that served the masters of the plantation here so long ago. It was not what most people would think of when they envisioned a plantation. "*Gone with the Wind*" had skewed history and made everyone think plantation houses were white-columned mansions with dozens if not hundreds of slaves and servants about. In North Carolina, most plantations were far more modest. They were truly working plantations where the master worked alongside the few slaves he could afford to scrape out a crop just enough to keep the place up.

When they reached the house, they took a break and took a seat on a small moss-covered hill looking out towards the lake. They broke out a few Slim Jim's and enjoyed the view and the quiet of the forest around them. Although several years of age separated the brothers, they were very close. They spoke most days and talked about everything. Because they were so close, Ricky was surprised when Bud broke the silence after a few moments.

"I have something that I want to tell you. I have wanted to for a long time, but for some reason, I just never felt like it was the right time." Ricky took a breath and felt a burst of butterflies in his stomach. "What could Bud have to tell me that I don't already know?" he thought.

Chapter 25

Bud took a breath and began his story. Ricky didn't need to be told the beginning of the story. Bud had met Michelle at his job at Phar-Mor Drug Store, and they had married as soon as Bud turned eighteen. Michelle had moved from Georgia to Durham to live with her mother and had stayed in North Carolina after her mom moved to South Carolina because she knew that Bud was the one for her. Michelle even moved into their sister Tracy's room until they could get married. When they did, Bud and Michelle moved into the cabin to start their lives together. It wasn't long after they were married that Bud had joined the military and left for his basic training. Ricky remembered the long drive to Cape May, New Jersey, to get Bud and bring him home from boot camp.

It was an exhausting day for everyone, especially Bud. Even though he was at the end of his basic training, he was officially a Coast Guardsman and had to be squared away one hundred percent of the time. It had been a tense and challenging two months for him, and he had seen himself grow and do things he never thought he could do. After the graduation ceremony, he loaded into the GMC Safari van with his wife and family. He headed south towards home for a short break before he reported to his first duty station. They passed through beautiful countryside as the van moved him closer to home, and he stared out of the window at the trees and fields as if he had not seen them in years instead of months. The last eight weeks had been so regimented and controlled. Every minute detail was scrutinized. Any mistake could bring any type of punishment or humiliation that the drill instructors could come up with.

When the van pulled into the dirt driveway that led to home, a wave of peace and nostalgia came over him, and he was, for the first time in a long time, entirely at ease. When he and Michelle finally got home to the little cabin, they were both totally worn out and soon went to bed. As tired as he was, though, Bud could not sleep. Bud was just so happy to be home that his mind raced as he stared at the ceiling. Bud pondered what the rest of their lives would look like and what it would be like for the next four years. It would be less stressful than the past eight weeks, he hoped. His body and mind craved sleep, but it would not come, but there in his own bed with his arm around his wife, Bud could care less. He was just glad to be home.

A faint, silvery glow of light shown in the kitchen doorway from a street light that his grandparents had installed years ago in front of their house. When they moved out to the country, the total darkness was hard to adjust to, so they had the power company come out and put up the light to provide a little comfort and security. The light was bright, and even over at the cabin, it lit up the kitchen at night just enough to cast faint shadows, but the big room where they slept remained dark. The white ceiling stood out in the darkness with this small amount of light, making it a pale cream color. Bud was glad he was not staring at the bottom of another bunk for a change.

As his mind wandered through the many new experiences they had in their near future, he suddenly felt the room become heavy. It was a weird feeling like someone had just walked into a room where everyone had been talking about them. It was an awkward feeling at first, but it drew his gaze away from the ceiling and into the doorway leading into the kitchen. There in the faint light bleeding in from the kitchen window, he could see something. His eyes focused in the darkness, and he saw something forming in the empty space past the door in the kitchen. It was misty but solid enough to block the light from coming through it. He sat up a little bit and stared at the form as it moved slowly towards him, stopping in the doorway between the kitchen and the big room that they slept in. At first, he thought it may be smoke, but as he focused on the shape, he knew it was not because of the way it moved.

He repositioned himself so that he could see the shape while trying not to disturb Michelle. She had fallen asleep as soon as they got into bed and was sleeping so soundly that he knew she had not slept well alone there while he was gone. The shape was slowly moving closer to them, and he could now see that it was definitely not smoke. The form moved as a single unit towards him, and then it stopped and seemed to grow darker. To Bud's horror, it continued to darken and in a matter of seconds was an inky black, bulbous figure floating just a few feet from them. The figure hovered there as if gazing upon them curiously. It seemed to pulsate, and he found himself frozen in horror, unable to move or speak. He could only stare in disbelief at this black mass that he could have only imagined seeing in a horror movie.

As Bud told Ricky the story, he looked straight ahead, afraid that his brother would think he was lying or crazy. They had shared many experiences, but nothing like this, and Bud knew the story was unbelievable. One glance over at his brother's face told him that he was feeling anything but skepticism. The look on Ricky's face was of terror as Ricky listened to his tale. It strangely comforted him as he continued.

The figure stood just a few feet from the end of their bed and seemed to stare at them as Bud stared back. Suddenly the figure spoke. "But not with words," Bud said. "It spoke directly to me…in my head." Again, he felt like he was talking crazy, but again, a look at Ricky's face betrayed no sign of disbelief.

"I came for her," the figure said. Bud looked down at his young wife sleeping there beside him, oblivious to what was happening. He looked back at the figure.

"No," Bud said in reply. Almost before the word had been uttered, the figure spoke again. Angrily and with so much force, Bud could practically feel the words.

"I CAME FOR HER!!!" the figure shouted as it began to move again towards them.

"NO! NO!" Bud yelled. "You can't have her!" Bud scooped Michelle up in his arms and held her tightly to his body. He realized at that moment the entity was there for his wife and was not going to stop until it had her. Bud also realized that he could not stop it himself. As Michelle began to awaken in his arms as he smothered her with his embrace, Bud began to call on the only power that he knew could stop what he now realized was a demon.

"In the name of Jesus Christ, Leave!" Bud shouted, "Leave!" Bud wrapped his other arm around Michelle, and she began to flail against him.

"No! You can't have her!" As he fought against his wife and called on the name of Christ, he could see the figure had stopped and was actually moving away from him. It retreated like smoke back through the doorway through the kitchen just as it had come in, dissipating as it left.

"Bud, you are having a nightmare!" Michelle yelled as he held her to his chest. She struggled out of his arms and looked at him.

"You were choking me. Are you ok?" she asked him.

Bud had no idea what to say to her.

"Yeah," he stuttered. "I thought I was still in boot camp," he lied.

Michelle put her arms around him and hugged him. "My Lord," she said, "What did they do to you?"

He never told Michelle what happened. Even as he was telling his brother about it so many years later, he still felt fear. Through all of the years that had passed since that night, working years as a Sheriff's Deputy and serving two combat tours in Iraq, he would never feel the same level of fear that he had felt that night. The fear stemmed from the total lack of understanding of what had happened. He had always feared that whatever it was would one day come back for Michelle. He had wanted to tell her a thousand times. He had wanted to tell Ricky a thousand times, but he could never tell his story until that day on the trail.

Chapter 26

Ricky took a deep breath. He remembered Michelle vividly telling everyone how Bud must have been "tortured" in boot camp because she woke up to being choked out by him the first night he was home. But to him, it was not just that tidbit that filled him with amazement at the story his brother had told him. Everything that Bud had told him he had already seen many times before. As Bud told him the story, Ricky could see the whole thing play out in front of him. He had seen it all from the perspective of his brother. He could see the entity form, and he saw it coming towards him. The fear that built up in him as the black figure neared him was always enough to wake him up. Ricky didn't hear anything in his dream, and he did not see Michelle, so he never knew that he was seeing things from Bud's perspective, but he had seen it all for sure. It was like Bud had been in his dream as he was telling him his story. In actuality, it was Ricky that had been in Bud's real-life nightmare.

Ricky could not understand how it could be that what Bud was describing was his very own nightmare that had plagued him for years. He also knew that Bud could not be making it all up. The only person in the entire world who knew about his nightmares was his wife Meghan, and he knew she had not told anyone about them. She was so very private about their lives that she would never speak about a personal matter like that with anyone. There was a better chance that Ricky would talk out of turn about private family matters, but Ricky knew he would not have told someone and then forgotten he had. He was incredibly embarrassed by the nightmares and would be mortified if someone knew that he, a grown man, was having bad dreams that shook him up so badly.

Bud continued with his story. He calmed Michelle down, and she soon fell back asleep, but he lay awake all night. He was on guard from whatever evil entity that he had encountered. Bud welcomed the sunlight as it peeked into the room through the window. When Michelle woke up, Bud had already made coffee and was packing for a quick trip they had planned to the mountains. He had a few days leave and honestly did not know how things would go after that. The military was not a nine-to-five job, and they wanted to take a little break before their new adventure started.

It had been a long night for Bud on top of a long day. Michelle asked him about his "dream" from the night before.

"I know it must have been a rough time, and it's understandable to have bad dreams," she said. He could tell that she was trying to make him feel better about what happened.

Bud appreciated her, and he wanted desperately to tell her what happened. However, he was still unsure how she would take it or even how to explain it to her. Basic training had been rough. It just sucks. Being away from home, being constantly harassed, and being constantly tense for eight weeks is really rough. He knew it was not brutal enough to make him have a nightmare even close to the experience he had last night, though. Nothing that he had experienced would have made him choke his wife in her sleep while yelling and screaming. He had no way of knowing it at the time. Still, Bud would later become a Navy Reservist and serve as a Combat Engineer, or Sea Bees, as they are known in the military. He would travel the world as a soldier and even serve in Iraq. Nothing Bud would ever see, including the horrors of war, would ever lead him to have a "dream" like that. The terror he experienced the night before was something that he would never again experience. Bud was just fine letting Michelle think he had a nightmare. He didn't want her to know, but then the phone rang.

Michelle's mother was on the phone calling from South Carolina. They were planning on stopping by her mother's house after their trip to the mountains, so Bud just assumed that she was calling to sure up the details. As he watched her though on the phone, he could tell something was wrong. Michelle leaned against the wall where the phone was and stared off into the living room. "No," she said into the phone. Bud sat up in his chair and watched her as she ran her hand through her hair and looked over at Bud.

"I don't want to talk to anyone about anything. I've been gone for almost two years," she said and then hung up the phone.

The stunned look on her face made Bud nervous, and he asked her what was wrong. She took a seat by him at the little table and told him what her mother had said. Michelle's mother had called because she had been contacted by the police department in the town they had lived in Georgia. Michelle's ex-boyfriend, who had broken up with her to date one of her friends, had driven to the girl's place of employment the night before and murdered her. He had walked in, shot and killed her, then went to his car in the parking lot and shot himself in the head. He had not died immediately but died in the hospital later that night. Apparently, he had left suicide notes to several people, including Michelle, and the police wanted to talk to her. She wanted neither the letter nor to speak to anyone about him.

Bud could tell that she was very shaken by what happened. Bud sat, contemplating the last few hours. He felt that whatever evil had made her ex-boyfriend kill his girlfriend, and then himself, had come there for Michelle. Bud was sure that it was a demon he had encountered the night before, looking there at his wife, who sat with her head in her hands beside him. He decided then that he would never tell her what really happened because he knew it would only scare her. He would carry the fear with himself alone for years, but it would never stray far from his mind.

When he had finished, Ricky sat stunned by not only the experience that Bud had, that somehow, he had seen also, but also by the rest of the story that Bud had told him. They sat in silence for a few minutes, and then Ricky told Bud that he had something to tell him. Ricky shared with him about the nightmare he had been having for years and how it was precisely what Bud had experienced that night. Bud was skeptical, and at first, thought Ricky was just messing with him. Ricky insisted, though, that he had seen it all. He could prove it. Meghan was at Bud's house while they were hiking. They had planned a cookout for later and were all going to meet back there after their hike. Ricky assured him that Meghan knew about the nightmare and would be able to tell him.

Chapter 27

Bud and Ricky emerged from the woods exactly where they started. Through the naked tree branches of late fall, the cabin appeared next to the red barn their great uncle had built for their granddad so many years ago. Moving up the hill, they walked in silence towards the homestead. Their grandparents' house became visible a few yards further as they neared the property. Drawing closer to the cabin, both men felt a kaleidoscope of emotions. Ricky felt the same uneasiness that he had felt for the cabin for the last few years, but he was also floored by the story that Bud had told him. How had he been dreaming something that had happened? How had he been able to see what Bud had seen? Was it just a coincidence? Bud felt relieved, having told someone. He knew he could never tell Michelle because even now, twenty years later, he thought it would terrify her.

They walked past the now abandoned cabin and trailer that had once been the focal point of their family many years ago. Trees grew out of the foundation, and moss grew on the sides of the now empty and cold homes. Up the hill, they went to the home of their youth. The house where their parents still lived seemed to be at the heart of their family. As they backed out of the driveway and headed towards Bud's house, they talked about all kinds of different things. What was on their minds was what Ricky's wife would say, though. Bud thought that Ricky was making fun of him and would make a big joke about it when he got to his house. He knew he would have to go along with him. The cat was out of the bag now. If Ricky walked in and started making fun of what he told him, he would have to pretend he made it all up or risk upsetting Michelle. "But what if he didn't?" he wondered. What would it mean if he had a dream for years about what Bud had seen?

Ricky had similar reservations. He was worried that Meghan would have forgotten his description of the nightmare. It had been a long time since he described it to her. She would always just ask him if it was the same dream when he had it. He also worried that she would say he didn't know what they were talking about. The brothers were known to rib her relentlessly, so she may think it was their way of messing with her and just say she had no idea what he was talking about. As they drove towards Raleigh, the unspoken anticipation was building and made the air in the car pregnant with the unknown.

When they arrived, they found the kids playing in the backyard on the swing set, and Michelle and Meghan were already prepping the food for the grill. Bud and Ricky made their way through the house, stopping to criticize as much of what their wives had done as possible in the short time it took them to get to the back deck. They took a seat and sat watching the kids play for a few minutes. Once Ricky saw that they would be left alone for the time being as the kids played, he walked back over to the backdoor and called inside to Meghan to come outside for a minute. He walked back over and took his seat beside Bud at the small glass patio table on the deck.

Meghan stuck her head out of the door. "Yeah," she said.

"Come here," Ricky said.

"What do you want?" she asked.

"I want you to come over here," Ricky said, becoming frustrated.

Meghan rolled her eyes and walked over to where they sat, expecting some form of hazing or nonsense from her husband and his brother.

"I need to help Michelle," she said as she stood over the two.

"Tell Bud about the dream I have," Ricky insisted.

She cocked her head to the side and looked at Ricky curiously. "What kind of game was this?" she wondered.

"Go ahead, it's ok," Ricky said. "Tell him everything you can remember."

Meghan sighed and took a seat on the other side of Bud. "You are talking about the nightmare you have, right?"

"Yeah. Tell him first how long I have been having it."

"Since I have known you," she said. Bud looked over at Ricky, already feeling even more uneasy than he had before.

"Ok, tell him about it if you can remember," Ricky said.

"From what I remember, you told me that you are in the cabin where you lived when you were little. Everything is dark except for the doorway to the kitchen, and you see a figure forming there. You watch it form into a solid black figure, and then it starts to move towards you. That is when you always wake up."

Ricky looked over at Bud to see his expression and could see the look of total shock on his face. He could tell that now that he had heard it from Meghan, he knew that Ricky had been being honest. But how in the world could it be? How could Ricky have seen what he saw? Bud knew he had never told anyone the story before.

"Why did you want me to tell him?" Meghan asked. "You always told me not to talk about it." Just then, the backdoor opened, and Michelle came bouncing across the porch.

"I'll tell you later," Ricky said, giving Meghan a look of secrecy.

"Ok, whatever," Meghan said, still expecting some form of foolishness from her husband.

To Ricky and Bud, their revelation became a source of so many more questions than answers. Was there some form of psychic telepathy going on between them? Had Bud wanted to tell him so bad that he had been sending out some signal to his brother? They would never be sure why, but they only knew what had happened. They both wondered if, somehow, they were sensitive to things like that. Maybe their experiences from their youth had opened up their senses to pick up on things that others tend to block out. They honestly didn't know for sure, but they did know that whatever explanation there was probably could be found somewhere in their past. It was most likely the influences from the little white farmhouse where they grew up and where they learned that there was more to the world than what you can see with your eyes and touch with your hands.

Chapter 28

"Family is a life jacket in the stormy sea of life."
-J.K. Rowling

Ricky and Meghan had been married for eight years when they decided to sell their two-story townhouse in Raleigh and move to a larger home in Wake Forest, which is just a little north of Raleigh. They had recently learned they were expecting their first child and decided to move out of town and get a house with a backyard and garage. Their new house fit the bill. It sat on a corner lot on a cul-de-sac and had a nice yard, and the neighborhood was great and full of small kids. Meghan had visions of their kids growing up with other kids in the neighborhood as she had done as a child in Baltimore. They settled in and began a happy life as they welcomed Savannah Grace into this world in November of the same year.

Everything about the home was so normal. It was built in the early nineties and was a typical suburban home. They had been there over two years when the first odd thing happened. Ricky worked at the bank and would get home after 6pm every day. He came home to a smiling baby girl and a loving wife one afternoon with dinner on the table waiting for him. It was a great way to begin to wind down after working all day. As they sat in the dining room and ate dinner, Meghan and Rick talked about their day, and Savannah played with her food in her high chair. She had made quite a mess, and Meghan sighed and said, "I guess I am going to take her straight up to the bath."

She picked Savannah up and walked up the stairs with her, and soon Ricky could hear the water turn on, and mama and daughter were talking and cooing back and forth. He usually sat at the head of the table, which looked across the dining room and into the kitchen. But, on this evening, because of where Meghan placed the high chair, he sat on the side of the table with the kitchen to his left.

As he finished his meal, he heard in the distance behind the house the sound of a fire engine siren. This was common because through the woods behind the house was a major road where fire engines and ambulances frequently passed on the way to a call. He didn't respond to the sound of the siren, but it tuned him into his surroundings because he began to hear another noise. A swishing sound was coming from the kitchen over his left shoulder. He looked into the kitchen and saw the lid to the trashcan swinging back and forth as if someone had pushed down hard on it. It swung several times, emanating the swishing sound as he watched it. Then it stopped.

When it stopped, another sound took its place. Footsteps began to fall on the kitchen floor, walking across the room from where the trashcan was to the area in front of the kitchen where he could not see from his position. They faded, and he was again left with only the sound of Meghan and Savannah laughing upstairs. There was no one else in the house but them, and he sat wondering how the trashcan could have moved and where the footsteps could have come from but was stumped. He did not feel nervous or scared, but he was perplexed by the event. Ricky thought it was better to keep it to himself and not tell Meghan. She worked from home, and he didn't want to make her uncomfortable.

Chapter 29

Strangely, Ricky got a call just a few days later at work from Meghan, and she was very upset about something that happened. She told him that she was working in the living room and began to hear scratching and chewing noises coming from the kitchen like a mouse was there. Meghan timidly got up and went in to investigate. She is not a fan of rodents and crept slowly across the room following the sound. It was coming from a cereal box that was sitting on the counter. It grew louder the closer she got to the box, and she could hear the mouse chewing and scratching the contents of the box. Usually, she would have left this task to Ricky, but since he was not home and wouldn't be for several more hours, she knew she had to do something. If she didn't, the mouse would eventually eat through the box and be loose in the house. She retrieved a large wooden spoon and approached the box as she steeled herself to what she had to do. She took the spoon and knocked the box over-prepared for the mouse to bolt out of the box, and when it did, she was going to whack it with the spoon. When she knocked the box over, though, the noise stopped, and silence fell on the house. She took the spoon and poked at the box. Again, it made no noise. Cautiously, she reached out and opened the box only to find that it was totally empty.

Ricky sat listening to her, remembering the strange occurrence he had experienced a few days earlier. He had finished the cereal that morning and had set the empty box on the counter, meaning to throw it in the recycling bin outside, but he had forgotten to take it out. When she had finished her story, Ricky told her what happened to him but with the caveat that she should not be too concerned. "These things just happen sometimes," he told her.

She was pretty shaken up about it, and she was even further bothered by what he told her. They had lived there for a few years, and nothing strange had happened before. They were really unsure what was going on, but they didn't really see anything that could or should be done about it. This was their second home, and nothing strange had ever happened in the other house. Was it the house, or was something attached to Ricky like a piece of gum on the bottom of his shoe, he wondered? These two events were not the last time that there would be odd occurrences in their house, though.

Another few days passed, and Ricky was surprised to find that their experiences were not done. His routine was the same for many years. He was an early riser and only depended on the alarm clock as a reminder to get out of bed and get going. Most mornings, he lay awake in bed, thinking about the day to come. When the kids came along, he usually found himself lying awake with a little foot in his face or in his side where one of the kids had snuck into their bed, making him uncomfortable and wishing the clock would go ahead and sound the alarm. He and Meghan were lax when it came to dragging the kids back to their own beds in the middle of the night and ended up often a threesome in the mornings. It started with Savannah. They had experienced some difficultly conceiving. She was such a miracle that they just didn't want to be separated from her. So, she snuggled up between them, and there they were. Whatever problems they had conceiving the eldest were somehow corrected after her birth because two more babies came in pretty rapid succession after she was born. When Meghan was pregnant with Ricky Junior, they knew it was time for Savannah to move into her own room.

It was harder for them than for her, and she took right to sleeping alone in her room. In fact, she was such a good girl about it that she would stay in her room and play even if she woke up before them. Many Saturday mornings, Ricky would wake up and go to her room to peek in on her, only to find her playing on the floor with her dolls smiling at him.

Just a few days after he and Meghan had their experiences in the kitchen, Ricky began his day and woke up like usual and headed out into the hall to check the thermostat. As the dad, it was his responsibility to police the thermostat and make sure that no one froze to death while also making sure they did not end up in the poor house because of the electric bill. Since he got up earlier than everyone else, his strategy was to crank the heat up right before Meghan woke up so that she would have the illusion of warmth at a discount price. As he passed Savannah's door, he heard her giggling. Ricky stopped and tiptoed closer, smiling. He pressed his ear to the door and heard her talking and laughing with her dolls. Ricky placed his hand on the door and slowly opened it expecting to see that bright smile flash in his direction to get him started on his day. What he found was unnerving. Savannah lay in her bed, mouth opened, drooling, and quietly snoring, lost in peaceful dreams.

He was disturbed as he stood by the door, looking down at his angel. Who was laughing and talking in her room? He saw and heard weird things all his life, but this was the first time anything came so close to his kids. Maybe he was going crazy? He closed the door and gave her a few more minutes of sleep before she had to get up for the day, but Ricky was shaken at the thought of what he had heard. It was not only the sound of laughing and talking coming from her room that bothered him, but the fact that it was distinctly that of a little girl. This troubled him greatly for very deep reasons. As a Christian, he believed that God has no wrath or judgment for a child who has not reached an age of accountability for sin. He had no idea what a "ghost" was, but he did know that the spirit of a child would not be wandering around the earth when Christ himself said they belong to Heaven.

Charlotte made three kids for the couple when she came along, and for Ricky, sleep became a thing of the past. He slept light and fell into a routine of making nightly security checks around the house after the kids went to sleep and before he and Meghan went to bed. He would usually get up at least once a night, go into the kid's rooms and look in on them. They had no trouble sleeping and were generally snoozing pretty well. The only living creature that would be stirring would be the cat who would sometimes dart in front of him as he made his nightly patrols, and it would scare the Hell out of him.

On one such night, they put the kids to bed and watched a little television. When they got ready for bed, Meghan went up first, and Ricky took their dogs out and did his usual walk around the house, checking the doors and making sure everything was in place. He walked up the stairs and found Meghan already tucked in bed. Their two little dogs trailed behind him up the stairs, and both jumped up on the bed to join Meghan while he went to the bathroom and got ready for bed. After his contacts were out and his teeth were brushed, he got into bed, shoving the dogs over on Meghan's side.

"Night, hun," he said as he pulled the covers over him.

BOOM!!!! They both sat upright in the bed at the crashing sound that came from downstairs. It was so loud and distinct that it undoubtedly came from the dining room. Follow-up sounds indicated the falling and rolling on the floor of other smaller items. Ricky bolted from the bed, quickly putting on his glasses as he took his gun from the nightstand beside the bed. He crossed the room in the darkness heading towards the door, fully expecting to find an intruder coming up the stairs. As a suspect, the cat was eliminated immediately as the sound was so big that the tiny gray cat could not have possibly caused anything that big to fall.

Meghan, obviously on the same page as him, trailed behind him as he exited the room. He stopped at the top of the stairs and looked down into the darkness. Meghan ran across the hall and into the girls' bedroom. Ricky waited as she ran out and further down the hall into Junior's room. Seconds later, he heard her say, "The kids are fine," and he began his descent of the stairs in the dark. Ricky strained his ears for any sounds that would give away the intruder's location, but there was only silence. When he reached the landing, he looked into the dining room, where he thought the sound must have come from since the living room was carpeted. The dark shadows of the night betrayed nothing out of place. Ricky moved towards the light switch and flicked it on, keeping his weapon ready for whatever the light revealed, but as his eyes adjusted, he could see the room just as he had left it.

He moved on into the kitchen and checked the garage. Absolutely nothing was out of place anywhere. He even walked outside and checked the surroundings of the house. No trees had fallen, and all of the neighbors' houses were dark. He came back inside and checked all of the rooms upstairs. He was so confused as he checked every room and found everything perfect. Meghan had checked everything upstairs as he had made his rounds. He even went into the attic only to find neatly stacked boxes and a bookcase full of old books. His heart was still beating as he and Meghan climbed back into bed to try to find sleep again. As they lay in the darkness, they finally talked about what had happened. They both heard the same crashing sound and had both been convinced that it had come from the dining room. Meghan confessed she was sure there was an intruder in the house and had gone back into their room and gotten her phone ready to call 911 as she listened at the top of the stairs for any sound of a confrontation. Ricky was baffled at the vividness of the sound of falling and rolling objects but found nothing out of place anywhere. Had it not been something they both had heard, he would have felt insane.

Chapter 30

Bedtime was always a fight. Getting the kids in bed was challenging, and often after Ricky and Meghan put them to bed, they would hear the pitter-patter of little feet coming down the stairs and then the plaintive voice of one of the kids saying they were hungry or thirsty or couldn't sleep. They would have to be walked back to bed and settled back down to make sure they got a good night's sleep to be able to face the upcoming day. On one of these extra challenging nights, both Ricky and Meghan had been taking turns putting the kids to bed and then putting them back in bed. Savannah was the last one up. As Ricky was leaving Junior's room after putting him back to bed for the hundredth time, he was met by Savannah in the hall.

"Daddy, I'm scared. Can I sleep in Ricky's room with him?"

"No, baby. He will just keep you up." He walked her back into her room and put her in bed.

"I'm scared, Daddy," she said again.

"Of what?"

"I don't know. I just feel like I am afraid," she said in a whiny voice.

"You are overtired, baby. I will leave your door open and our door open, ok? We are just right across the hall, ok?"

"Ok," she said, and although he could tell that she was scared, she rolled on her side facing the wall, and he leaned down and kissed her on her head.

"Goodnight, love you," Ricky said.

"Love you too," Savannah replied in a sleepy voice.

Ricky came into the room and found Meghan still awake snuggled up to Charlotte, who had snuck in and was already asleep.

"Is everything ok?" she asked.

"Oh yeah, they're good. Love you," he responded.

"Love you, too," Meghan said and snuggled down in the comforter as Ricky took his glasses off and set them on the nightstand beside the bed. In no time, he could hear the gentle snoring of Meghan, who had never had trouble falling asleep beside him. Ricky was a light sleeper and lay there in bed, listening to the sounds of the house. He could hear crickets chirping outside of the window and the dog snoring in the corner loudly. A gentle wind blew against the windows of his bedroom. As he was slipping into sleep himself, he suddenly became aware of the sound of footsteps in the hall outside of his bedroom door. He opened his eyes and saw the crack of faint light coming into his room from the night light in the hall.

"Who is up now?" he thought as he reached for his glasses next to him.

"Who's there?!" he heard Savannah say frantically from her room. It startled him so much that he fumbled the glasses and dropped them on the floor beside his bed. He threw himself after them and was in an instant, putting them on as he burst through the door and into the hall.

"Daddy," she called out to him.

He was in her room in a flash and found her in her bed with the covers pulled up around her face looking at him with eyes like saucers.

"Daddy, I heard someone walking in my room," she said, holding back tears.

Ricky looked around at the empty room and leaned back out into the hall to find it empty also.

"Was it your brother?" he asked.

"No, I couldn't see anyone, but I heard it."

Ricky walked down the hall and looked into Junior's room, where he was fast asleep in a tangle of blankets, pillows, and stuffed animals. He went back down the hall to Savannah's room.

"You were probably just dreaming, honey," he said, not daring to tell her that he had heard the footsteps too. "There is nothing here. Everything is ok."

"Ok," she meekly replied. Savannah was a daddy's girl, and she trusted him. So, if daddy said it was ok, then she was inclined to believe him. Ricky sat on her bed and kissed her again on her head.

"Go to sleep, ok," he said as he rubbed her back. He sat with her until she was asleep, but he was listening intently for any sounds. The house had fallen back into the routine of sounds present before the footsteps came - snoring, crickets, and wind. It was not until she was fully asleep that he went back to bed and tried to get some sleep himself, not to be bothered again for the night.

Chapter 31

Kathy and Robert enjoyed their time alone together in the homeplace. Their kids were married, and they had plenty of grandchildren coming and going. Everyone lived close by, and they could see everyone often, but they had one more dream to follow. They had one more adventure to go on together, and that was to move to the coast. They began in earnest thinking about the move looking at houses and making plans. When they finally made up their minds to do it, they sold the house to Bud. He always had the deepest connection to the homeplace and wanted to finish raising his family there in the place where he had been raised.

The last Christmas in the house for Robert and Kathy was a bitter-sweet one. They had not found a place to buy yet, but the decision was made, and they had already sold the house to Bud. One last time the family met there to share the holidays together. Smells of turkey, ham, all of the sides, and Kathy's chocolate meringue pie filled the house along with laughter and loud voices talking over each other. The kids laughed and played, running in and out of the house to the annoyance of Robert. The small house was full of discarded wrapping paper and gifts the kids had opened and soon abandoned to play with their cousins in the chilly December air outside.

The adults settled into different rooms to spread out and talk about their Christmas plans and whatever else crossed their minds. Soon they had all crowded into the living room, and a round-robin conversation began of memories of Christmases past. They talked about spending Christmas Eve with Papa and Granny in their trailer that still sat just a short distance down the hill but was now cold and dark inside. Ricky remembered standing with the big kids outside as they talked about things he could barely understand. Still, they seemed to let him tarry because it was Christmas. He could remember no other time he was so accepted into the older kids' sacred circle, so that must have been the cause.

Behind the celebration, though, was an unspoken sadness. They all knew that this was the last time, the last memory they would make here together. It was just like so many Christmas Eves they had spent in the little trailer with Granny and Pop when their house was warm and vibrant just as their home was now. They also shared memories of going to Granny Tripp's house, where family flooded in and out all day. Ricky and Tracy stealthily snuck potato candy and cookies from the Christmas tins when they thought no one was looking. Like all of those memories, they all knew that everything had a beginning and an ending, and this was the end of this tradition.

As Bud stood in the doorway leading from the living room into the kitchen, taking it all in one last time, he suddenly felt a tap on his shoulder snapping him out of his trance-like state. He turned and saw his oldest daughter Anna. Now a grown woman and married herself, she had a look on her face Bud was still familiar with. It was a look he had seen a hundred times when there was a boogeyman in the closet or something under the bed. She was scared!

"What's wrong?" he asked as she motioned for him to come into the kitchen. He followed her, and she looked around back over his shoulder as if to tell him some secret that no one else should hear.

"It's gone now," she said as she breathed in heavily.

Confused, he asked, "What is?"

"The man," she said, "I smelled the man." Bud realized what she was talking about immediately and took a big whiff. All he could smell were the leftovers and other Christmas smells. She told him that she had gone to the bathroom and then stood in the kitchen for a few minutes watching the kids play outback. She was thinking about getting a piece of pie and joining the other adults in the living room when she was stopped in her tracks by the sudden smell of dirt and body odor that swept over her. She stood still for a moment, not realizing what was happening. It was distinct, but she was alone. Not only alone but alone surrounded by all of these wonderful smells.

Bud listened intently and then told her that it was just the ghost popping in for the holidays, but he could tell she was freaked out. It was a reminder that no matter how the activity seemed to lessen in the house, it never completely dissipated. As they went back into the living room and took their place among the family elders, Bud looked back over his shoulder and wondered if he was making the right decision by moving in with his family. He hoped that the activity didn't increase, but he was committed now and intended to make it work no matter what.

Chapter 32

Bud and Michelle moved into the old house in a whirlwind of change and elbow grease. Thirty years of accumulated memories were stacked in the house's corners and closets and had to be dealt with. Robert and Kathy took what they prized the most and moved it to their beach condo. All the other items had to be gone through by Bud and Ricky to see if they wanted anything. Tracy had recently moved with her family to Colorado so she was not in a position to help. When the culling was complete, Bud and Michelle made countless trips to the second-hand store and the dump, clearing out all of the stuff left behind. The empty shell of the house had to be painted and repairs made before they could move in with their family. All the while, through all of those long hard days of work getting the house ready, Bud could not help but remember his dad and mom working long hours many years ago to get the home prepared for them. He also remembered the strange occurrences that had seemed to spring from the woodwork upon moving into the house many years ago. He wondered if the renovations would wake something that was dormant there.

After living in the house for over a year, they both felt whatever saturated the house before had dried up. They went about their lives in regularity and looked at a future of enjoying the country home that had been their home long before they lived there, it seemed. So much hope was put into the little house as Bud and Michelle began to see the end of their time having kids at home. Their oldest daughter was married, and their second oldest was in college. They had a middle schooler and a fourth-grader. They could see an empty nest in their near future.

Once the house was empty, they began any repairs that were needed. Like any house that has been lived in for so long, it needed a fresh coat of paint and some tender loving care. Bud would bring a change of clothes, and when he got off of work, he would change out of his uniform and into some cargo shorts to paint or clean. He would often work alone until late into the evening when fatigue would force him to his current house for food and rest to get ready for the next day.

One evening he came in from work and sat his gym bag containing his change of clothes on the floor beside the door. He planned on grabbing a drink out of the refrigerator, eating a quick snack, and getting straight to work. The finish line was in sight, and he wanted to get everything done as soon as possible to get settled in. He had a friend who helped do some of the work and decided he would go upstairs really quick to see what he had gotten done. When Bud got to the bottom of the stairs, the same smell of dirt and body odor wafted over him like a breeze from upstairs. It passed over him and was gone in a moment as if he had passed someone on the stairs. He looked over his shoulder and then back up the stairs.

"Not tonight," he thought and decided that it could wait. He grabbed his bag and headed home. The next day, when he spoke to his friend, he asked Bud if he had ever had anything weird happen in the house before. Bud said that he had. His buddy told him that he heard a knocking sound upstairs when he had been working in the house the day before. It was almost like a ball bouncing, but he could never find anything when he went up to check it out. Bud just smiled. "If you have a minute, I could tell you a story or two."

He was amazed as he listened to Bud tell him story after story of the strange encounters in the house. He was a true skeptic and didn't believe in ghosts at all, but he had to admit that he could not identify what he had heard the day before. Maybe there was something funny going on, he acknowledged but stopped just short of attributing it to the paranormal. Either way, they agreed that the show had to go on, and there was a little more work to be done.

Michelle met Bud later that day at the house when he got off to finish painting upstairs. As they ascended the stairs with Michelle leading the way and Bud following her, Bud suddenly stopped. Behind him, he heard a third set of footsteps on the stairs. Bud spun around, not even considering the possibility of a ghost because of the sound's vividness. When he turned around, he expected to find a physical person standing there, but he found an empty staircase. He turned back up the stairs and looked at Michelle, who was looking at him.

"What's wrong?" she said.

"Did you hear the footsteps behind us?" he asked.

She looked at him quizzically and then scoffed. "You're crazy!" she said and turned back up the stairs and was on her way. After all of these years, he thought, she is still doubting the house is haunted. Or possibly she is just hoping he is wrong. He would be hopeful himself as that was the last incident they experienced for the rest of the remodel and even after moving into the house. The kids were happy, and they were pleased spending time outside working the land and tending their garden they planted. There was always something to be done, it seemed, and it kept them busy.

Chapter 33

The rain was coming down in sheets as Bud peered out of the front window. The lightning flashed and illuminated the flood of water washing across the entire driveway and lawn. There were huge puddles and standing water all around the house. He cursed the mud that he knew would take forever to dry up in the shade of the tall oak trees. He could already see the kids' muddy footprints that he knew would be a problem for at least a week or two. As the storm worsened, he and Michelle walked around the house, lighting candles in anticipation of the power going out. The last thing they wanted to have to do was to stumble around through the darkness to find the kids. There was no ambient light in the country, so if the power went out, they knew it would be pitch black, and the girls would be scared or try to make it down the stairs, which could be very dangerous.

Sure enough, the lights flickered and then went out as they were lighting the last candles. For the next hour, they spent time together in the candlelight like many other families for over a hundred years had done in that house. They talked and laughed and got ready for bed. Bud and Michelle took the kids to bed, and Bud made sure that all of the lights in the house were turned off. He knew the power would come on sometime overnight, and it would wake everyone up. As he got into bed himself, the house was ink black and silent. Although the storm had passed, the night remained cloudy and moonless.

Around midnight, Bud sat up in bed, realizing that something was wrong. His eyes could not open despite the need to see what was wrong. As he squinted his eyes open, he realized that what was wrong was that in his haste to turn off all of the lights in the house, he had neglected to turn the lights off in their room. The sudden flood of light had woken him up. As his eyes adjusted, he looked over at Michelle, who looked back at him through half-closed eyes and pulled the pillow over her head.

"Dang, I must have forgotten to cut our lights off."

"Really?" she asked sarcastically.

She rolled out of bed and headed to the bathroom as Bud got out of bed to close the windows and make sure the air conditioning was on. Although it was fall in North Carolina, that is just part two of summer, and the nights were still warm. He walked through the entire house checking everything, and found Michelle back in bed waiting for him when he made his way back to their room.

"Let's try this again," he said as he cut off the lights and crawled in bed. They talked for a few moments before sleep again began to creep upon them. In the dark and silence that again had descended upon the house, Bud began to hear Michelle's faint breathing. He lay awake, assuming that she had fallen asleep already. Years of the military and law enforcement made sleep harder to come by than his wife, and he sighed wondering when, and if, sleep would come. Soon his ears perked in the darkness as a loud whisper from a female voice caught his attention.

It was obviously coming from the doorway to his room, which was opened. He couldn't make out what the voice was saying, but it was a constant stream of words coming from the darkness.

"What was that!?" Michelle said suddenly from his side, sitting up in the darkness.

"It sounded like a woman whispering," Bud said as he sat up too.

"Exactly," she said, "I thought it was Mackenzie."

Bud thought it was his youngest daughter also when he first heard it and had been waiting for her to appear at their bedside. But the room was empty, and there were no footsteps or sounds of movement throughout the house at all. Bud got out of bed and turned the light on again. He rechecked the house but found everything as he had left it just a short while before. Bud spent the rest of the night fitfully trying to sleep. He lay awake much of the night listening for any other sounds, but he heard nothing. Michelle snuggled up close to him with her head under the covers the rest of the night. He wondered if there had been something to the conditions around the house - the storm, the lightning, the candles, the darkness. Whatever combination could have triggered some entity to wake up and make itself known to them once more after all of this time?

Epilogue

The Jackson family is more spread out than it has ever been since they left Ireland's shores for the new world. The family of five that once slept in the same room of a small cabin in the woods now live from the Rocky Mountains to the Atlantic Ocean. Robert and Kathy sit in side-by-side chairs in their condo and watch their old shows together - *Bonanza, Gunsmoke,* and all of the classics. They watch these shows and reminisce about the old days. How many times had these episodes come on over the years, and they could not watch them because they had to work, or had to cut grass, or had the kids to deal with. Days and nights once seemed to fly by as their kids grew and became adults right before their eyes. Now the days have slowed to a crawl, and they cherish their times together and their crazy younger days when it seemed that they had a million things to do and a hundred places to be.

Ricky and his family live near to the old homeplace in a neighborhood in the suburbs. He and Meghan have grown their roots deep into the area and envision their children one day living near and being a part of the same community that they have lived in together for years. Tracy and Jeremiah have moved with their four children to Colorado. Always the rebel, she could not resist the pull of the call of the west that has drawn many people for so long. "Go west, young man" was the call after the Civil War. Still, the same feeling of new beginning and opportunity exists today and drew them there to build a better life and provide more opportunities for their kids.

Bud has been the anchor to the past in the Jackson family. He moved into the old farmhouse with Michelle and his two youngest children. Like a lighthouse keeper, Bud tends the light there. The history of the family runs through his veins, and he holds each memory dear. The family house is a beacon for all of the others. Calling for them to come back, to come home from their travels to the place where the Jacksons have been for so very long. The light grows weaker for the scattered family as they build their lives elsewhere, but it still calls to them. Even one day, when the light is extinguished, as long as one of the kids live, they will not be able to deny the importance of the house in their lives. The happy memories will remain along with the sad ones. The laughs and the tears will be there too. Somewhere past all of those memories will always be the ghosts.

About the Authors

Rick and William Jackson both graduated from Campbell University and co-authored the book Ghosts of the Triangle. Rick obtained his MBA from Mount Olive University and teaches high school economics and business classes and William is retired from the military and law enforcement.

www.ingramcontent.com/pod-product-compliance
Lightning Source LLC
LaVergne TN
LVHW050641100826
845148LV00011B/1943

* 9 7 8 1 7 3 6 6 1 3 0 0 9 *